The Runner's Book

DATE DUE			
MAY 6 - 1981			
MAY 26 1981			
SEP 29 1981			
AUG 30 1982			
OCT 8 1982			
DEC 7 1982			
AUG 29 1983			
OCT 4 1983			
NOV 9 1983			
AUG 1 5 1985			

WILLIAMSTOWN PUBLIC LIBRARY

BOOKS BY RAYMOND BRIDGE

The Complete Snow Camper's Guide

America's Backpacking Book

Freewheeling: The Bicycle Camping Book

*The Camper's Guide to Alaska, The Yukon,
    and Northern British Columbia*

Tourguide to the Rocky Mountain Wilderness

Climbing: A Guide to Mountaineering

*High Peaks and Clear Roads: A Guide for Safe
    and Easy Outdoor Skills*

The Complete Guide to Kayaking

The Complete Canoeist's Guide

The Runner's Book

THE RUNNER'S BOOK

Raymond Bridge

CHARLES SCRIBNER'S SONS · NEW YORK

Dedicated to Mike and Anne Fenerty,
runners and good friends

Library of Congress Cataloging in Publication Data
Bridge, Raymond.
    The runner's book.

    Bibliography: p.
    Includes index.
    1. Jogging. 2. Running. I. Title.
GV494.B74   796.4'26   78-18747
ISBN 0-684-15742-X
ISBN 0-684-15869-8 pbk.

1 3 5 7 9 11 13 15 17 19   V/C   20 18 16 14 12 10 8 6 4 2
1 3 5 7 9 11 13 15 17 19   V/P   20 18 16 14 12 10 8 6 4 2

PRINTED IN THE UNITED STATES OF AMERICA

Contents

Introduction

Shortly after returning from a trip east to run the Boston Marathon, I took a run near home along one of my favorite routes. After about fifteen minutes on the roads, I turned onto a trail that climbs up for a couple of miles through meadows and groves of Ponderosa pine before it intersects another trail, one that winds along the base of the rock formations dominating the area. Spring had arrived during my absence, and sand lilies and bluebells were in bloom along the trail, distracting my attention from the strain of the unremitting two-thousand-foot climb. As I broke into a meadow, a couple of deer looked up with mild interest but decided that I couldn't run fast enough to pose any threat and went back to grazing. A towhee called from a nearby bush as a cloud drifted across the sun, providing a little welcome shade and a brief afternoon shower to cool me for the last mile of steady uphill.

Soon after the shower stopped, I finished the hard climb as I came out onto the undulating trail that traverses the foothills near my home. From this point the uphill grades are interspersed with flat sections of trail and downhill intervals, so the runner can increase the pace and enjoy the scenery more. Everything had turned a rich green since the last time I had run the trail, and the contrasting colors of the vegetation, blue sky, and red rock stood out vividly against the puffy white afternoon cumulus clouds. It was a perfect run, a dream run in which the effort of the muscles heightened rather than dulled my awareness of the surroundings: an interval of beauty and clarity, of unity between the mind and the body.

Such times must contribute to the joy that so many people find in running and to the motivation of the hundreds of thousands of Americans who run or jog regularly. The joy of running has itself taken on great importance for many who began jogging for fitness.

The U.S. Running Explosion

A few years ago, practically nobody in the United States ran, except for children, commuters trying to catch a bus, and competitors in high school and college track. There have always been a few eccentrics, of course, who ran for training or pleasure, but they were sufficiently rare to be considered in the same general category with those wearing long robes and carrying signs proclaiming the imminent end of the world. Almost everyone who has been running for very long has a collection of stories about encounters with suspicious and unbelieving police officers. Even men who ran competitively in school rarely continued after graduation, and competitive women's running, particularly long-distance events, scarcely existed until recently.

All that has changed. Running has grown at a rate that can accurately be called phenomenal. Whereas a few years ago the sight of an early-morning runner was remarkable, today one can hardly go out in many towns and cities at dawn without seeing runners on the sidewalks and streets and in parks; runners' shoes and warm-up suits are now copied by mass-marketing specialists and sold for leisure wear.

No one knows how many people in the country run or jog regularly, because running is a fundamentally anarchic activity. No special facilities are needed; no one's permission or sanction has to be obtained, and one can run virtually anywhere, anytime. Most people who run do so outside of organized programs and are therefore difficult to count. Even competitive running needs only a minimum of organization, except at the level of world-class athletes. This is especially true for road races over long distances, because there are roads everywhere. Indeed, it is precisely in distance running, formerly the most neglected area of the sport, where the most interest has sprung up. Young school children and octogenarians can be found all over the country running five, ten, and fifteen miles a day. Many of them regularly compete in the thousands of road races that have been organized in the last few years.

We know more about the growth of competitive running because it is by its nature more organized. Ken Young of the National Running Data Center has statistics on forty thousand Americans who finished long-distance races in 1975 and fifty-five thousand in 1976, a growth rate that seems to be continuing. These figures include only races longer than fifteen kilometers (nine miles).

Marathoning is illustrative of the tremendous growth in participation and ability in U.S. distance running. The marathon, a race of 26 miles, 385 yards, has become the classic race for distance runners. A U.S. runner in the early 1950s would probably not have been able to find a half-dozen marathon races in the entire country; the only two with a long tradition are those in Boston and Yonkers, New York. By the early sixties there were about a dozen. In 1977 there were approximately 175, and the number of people finishing marathons exceeded twenty thousand. At Boston the classic U.S. marathon (it has been run continuously since 1897 except for one year during World War I), the number of entries has become so large that officials have had to limit the number of entrants to maintain a semblance of control. Even with stringent limitations, there were over three thousand official entrants and probably more than a thousand unofficial ones in 1977. At least thirty-four hundred finished.

The running population has grown from a handful of eccentrics to a group numbering in the millions. The reasons are many: running costs very little, it can be done almost anywhere, and it's fun!

Why Run?

Most runners do not enter races, or at least have no thought of doing so when they begin running. Even for most racers, the motivation for running is not the possibility of winning, since very few of the people who run races regularly have any illusions about placing near the winner. The goals and rewards sought by most runners are personal ones. The runner finds some combination of health, relaxation, aesthetic satisfaction, and a feeling of physical and mental wholeness that is sufficient to justify the time and effort that running requires.

Most of the people who join the throngs of runners every year are new to running. The majority have never run any significant distance before. A few runners will have begun in school, so that even if their running careers were interrupted, they have experience on which to draw and probably at least some happy memories. Generally, however, schools have left most people with unpleasant impressions of running that most new runners have to overcome, along with the poor physical condition in which most Americans find themselves. The U.S. running explosion is all the more amazing if one is aware of the difficulties that have to be overcome by the average person who makes up his or her mind to start running. The dropout rate is very high, but it is surprising how many people have broken through the initial barriers and reached the stage where running becomes truly enjoyable.

For most neophytes the motivation to start running or jogging is physical fitness. Some want to lose weight and regain muscle tone, some are worried about heart attacks or have had them and want to recover, and some would simply like to be in better condition. Those who manage to stick with their running for a while begin to find all sorts of benefits, and talking to a confirmed runner is often a little like encountering a proselytizer for a religious cult. Many of these advantages, both hypothetical ones and those with demonstrated validity, will be discussed in detail later, but because fitness is the normal motivation for beginning running, it must be considered first.

Running is one of the best ways of achieving and maintaining general physical fitness. Swimming or bicycling might be better for some individuals because of special circumstances, and there are other activities that can be equally valuable, but the special advantages of running give it preeminence.

The most important fitness is that of the breathing and circulatory systems, which deliver a constant supply of oxygen to the tissues of the body and carry away carbon dioxide. Body cells must be supplied with oxygen and other nutrients from the blood and have waste products washed out or they will cease to function and die. The more efficiently this system of supply and cleansing works, the more easily the organism can carry out daily tasks and the higher its capacity for hard work. Cardiopulmonary fitness is the most important requisite for good health and a feeling of physical well-being.

The body tends to strengthen itself to meet the demands that are placed on it and to weaken in those areas that are left unused and allowed to atrophy. If it does not stretch and move, it becomes stiff and inflexible. If muscles are not put under stress, they become weak. However, regular exercise stimulates the body to develop strength in those areas that are subjected to stress. Thus, to develop or maintain powerful and efficient hearts, lungs, and circulatory systems, we have to make them work hard. The sort of work that is needed is extended effort, because there is no point in developing a capacity for one or two strong heartbeats followed by a rest. The heart has to keep on beating, so the only kind of meaningful training for the heart is endurance training. To develop good cardiopulmonary fitness, one needs exercise that places the breathing and circulatory system under mild stress for a period of time. Exercise to develop cardiopulmonary fitness needs to be steady and to require enough effort to make the heart, lungs, and blood vessels work. Any vigorous activity that continues for a long enough period will do: walking, swimming, running, cycling, cross-country skiing, and other sports that keep the body moving.

The special advantages of running as a conditioning exercise are that it can be done with or without companions, that it nearly always is vigorous enough to produce the needed demands on the body, that no special facilities are needed, that it can be done almost anytime and anywhere, and that there are therefore few good excuses for not getting enough exercise to keep yourself healthy.

Running has disadvantages too, which are the cause of the

high dropout rate among people who take up jogging for fitness. The greatest objection to running for exercise is that many people find it hard to get started. For many of us, running becomes enjoyable only after we have run for some time and are running a considerable distance each day. Running is also more likely to cause excessive stress in the joints than more fluid activities such as swimming, cycling, and cross-country skiing. One of the main purposes of this book is to help some of the people who take up running for fitness to get through the initial difficulties that cause so many to quit before they have had time to gain some of the benefits of regular running.

What This Book Is About

This book is divided into two main parts, the first oriented toward beginners and the second directed to people who have been jogging or running for a while. The differentiation is only a rough one, but the problems of the two groups do tend to be different, despite a natural overlap. The beginner is more likely to be concerned with getting through his or her first few miles, whereas the person who has been at the sport a bit longer may be thinking about a first marathon. The novice who has spent twenty sedentary years in the office has to worry about putting too much strain on the heart, whereas the veteran of a couple of marathons is more concerned about straining the Achilles tendons.

For the beginner this book has two main goals: to help promote enjoyment of running and to help people avoid injury. Unless you enjoy running, you probably will not keep it up; you will quit out of boredom or disgust. Thus, whether you are starting running for pleasure or fitness, it is important to have a good time; otherwise, you will probably attain neither. You may not love every run you take—there are bound to be times when your only goal is to get through the run—but the overall experience has to be positive. One of the difficulties in beginning running is that the hardest months are the first ones. I hope this book will help you through them.

A common problem of both beginning and experienced runners is that they tend to go at things too hard. Most injuries result

The growth in competitive distance running on the roads has paralleled the enormous increase in running generally. The Boston Marathon, America's classic road race, has had to limit entries but still had over 3,000 runners in the 1977 race. After 21 miles, Peter Nye, Anthony Rodiez, and Robert Bunfan are running at a pace of about 6:25 minutes per mile.

from impatience, from overstress, from ignoring warning signs. This is as true of world-class runners as it is of joggers in the park. It is especially important for the recreational runner and the person seeking fitness to be cautious, however.

Your goals, if you think about them, are long-term ones: fitness five years from now and twenty years after that. Running allows you to place on your body almost any level of stress you choose, which is a great advantage if it is used wisely, but you will hurt yourself if you overdo things. Running is a great teacher, but it can be a harsh one. If you have been busy getting out of shape for thirty years, you will not get back into condition in three weeks, no matter what miracle solution you try. Running will allow you to achieve a level of fitness that is probably far greater than you can imagine, but it will not offer instant solutions. Train for a race ten years from now and the rewards will start to come sooner than you think.

The second part of this book includes a good deal of information on particular kinds of training, injuries, exercises, and so on for the experienced runner. The emphasis is on distance running, particularly running on trails and roads. Serious competitors interested in doing a 3:45 mile or a 2:05 marathon have plenty of coaching and theoretical material available to them, and this book is intended for those whose goals do not include gold medals, for the moment at least. Distance running is better suited for general conditioning and less likely to cause injury than running short distances, as well as being of more interest to recreational runners.

I hope this book will prove useful to some of my fellow runners and that it will help those who are just starting to find the same satisfaction in running that I have enjoyed.

I am particularly grateful to Dr. Rob Roy McGregor and his colleagues and patients at Deaconess Hospital and Braintree Hospital for the many hours they spent with me at the runners' clinics in the Boston area.

PART 1

MAINLY
FOR
BEGINNERS

1 / *Running for Fun*

Running should be recreational in the broadest sense of the word: the runner should feel re-created after the run—physically refreshed, mentally relaxed, and emotionally reinvigorated. Have a good time when you are running and the more superficial and more profound effects will follow. Neither conditioning effects nor relaxation can be forced, but both will come more quickly if you are having fun when you run.

How can running be fun? It is, after all, hard, sweaty work. Distance running in particular is generally associated with drill sergeants and physical-education teachers who taught many of us to abhor running. Coupled with unpleasant memories is the fact that running doesn't feel very good until the body has become accustomed to it. The worse shape one is in, the more this tends to be so. By working up to the desired distance and speed slowly, however, a lot of the discomfort associated with beginning running can be avoided. Even powerful runners start off at a slow pace or a walk at the beginning of a run, to allow the muscles to warm up before stressing them, and this principle of gradually increasing the intensity of effort is still more important over the long term.

Few people should begin a running program with a run at all. Most should start with intermittent jogging and walking or with walking alone. (The next chapter discusses starting routines in detail.) The important point is that the starting steps of a running program do not have to be strenuous and painful. The muscles have to be stressed to persuade them to tune themselves, but straining them will set progress back rather than speed it. You can start enjoying yourself from the start of your running (even if you aren't running yet), but you have to keep your expectations in check to do so. Plan to enjoy each day at the level of fitness you have now.

You will soon find it getting better and will be amazed at the progress you make over the months. If you set your hopes too high, however, and secretly expect to be loping effortlessly over the miles within a couple of weeks, you are bound to be disappointed, and you'll probably either try too hard or quit. Start enjoying your daily walk or jog for its own sake and the improvements will take care of themselves.

The Joy of Running

I recently visited a wildlife sanctuary on the Atlantic coast, near which I used to live. Running there is still fresh in my mind: it is a beautiful spring day, with a cool gusty wind blowing out of the northwest, but a bright warm sun shines down on the light-colored sand beach. The sky is a vivid blue of the kind that is becoming rare in the Northeast, with an occasional puffy cloud, condensed out of moisture drawn up by the sun from ground still wet after a week of rain, and sent scudding out to sea by the wind. A line of breakers extends into the distance parallel to the sand of the beach and the green vegetation growing behind on the higher dunes. Loons that have not yet started north fish just outside the line of breaking waves. Farther out to sea a raft of scoters appears briefly on the crest of a wave and then falls from view again.

Living as I do by the Rocky Mountains, I have not seen the Atlantic for a long time, and I have anticipated the run along this beach for months. I cut diagonally through the dunes toward the water, forced to work hard immediately to make progress in the soft sand, even though my pace is relatively slow. As I reach the water's edge, I experiment with running at various distances parallel to the pulsing line of the incoming waves. There is a hard section of sand that has been dampened by the waves just enough so that the water acts more like cement than a lubricant. I need all the help I can get because running in sand can be very strenuous, pleasant as it is, and I still have twelve miles to go. Alas, the sand grains on this section of the beach are too large to pack well, so there is no way to cheat. My feet sink in at every step, and I have to work hard for the next half mile.

The running is superb. At home I run either on rough trails or on roads, usually paved. In the yielding sand, I can run barefoot with no worries: it is still too early in the year for the litterers to have added fresh broken glass to the sand, and the action of the waves over the winter rubs the sand incessantly against last year's supply of glass, rounding off the edges and rendering them harmless. I'm not sure how long my tender skin will last, however, so I carry my shoes in my hands.

After the first five minutes or so, still wandering up and down the fluctuating edge of the water, sometimes on dry sand and then through a subsiding wave, I find more substantial footing as the texture of the sand alters to slightly smaller grains. The shape of the beach is ever changing, a shifting truce line between the forces of wind, water, and anchoring vegetation. The profile of the sand varies from season to season and from one hundred-yard stretch to another. Where I am running, the sand at the water's edge drops steeply, and the constant angle is hard on the ankles, but I know from past experience that the incline will be more gradual a couple of miles up the beach, unless there have been radical changes in the island during the last few years. It will also be less steep later this summer, as the influence of the violent northeast winter storms dissipates. My highway extends along the strip that is damp from the highest waves but is above the point that most of them are able to reach; gravity drags them back just below my feet. The surface of this narrow and shifting strip is perfect. As my heel strikes, it sinks perhaps half an inch, cushioning the shock that paved surfaces unremittingly transmit back through all one's joints. The outer edge of the foot drops down, sinking in only a little as it lets the ball of the foot roll down onto the ground. The toes, curled up as the foot descended, now drop and bite into the sand to drive off. Everything speeds up as soon as I reach this harder strip of sand paralleling the water's edge. The running feels smooth, fast, and exhilarating—not effortless, but never straining, either—as it does on those perfect days that capture the essence of running, the runs that you try to keep uppermost in your mind on mornings when it is a major victory to struggle out onto the street and start moving.

The beach reveals itself like a scroll, unwinding in the distance ahead and rolling back up behind, a strip of sculpted sand and breaking waves, bordered on one side by the North Atlantic and on the other by the boundless sky. Along the watery line of demarcation are the feeding birds, eager for the fresh morsels being brought in by the sea. Grebes swim behind the breaker line, disappearing occasionally as they dive for food. Ahead there must be an irregularly shaped section of shoreline, because a whole flock of gulls is gathered along one little bit of beach, where incoming debris must be concentrated by the shape of the bottom. The difference in contour is small, but its importance for the birds is enormous, like the difference for me in the size of the sand grains washed to various parts of the beach. Most of the watchful group is made up of herring gulls of various ages, but a couple of great black-backed gulls stand out with special dignity on the fringes, twice the size of the others and striking with their very dark backs and pure white heads and breasts. The group shifts constantly, most of the gulls watching the waves break, a few taking off and flying into the spray of each wave as they spot some morsels of food in the foam.

Along the other boundary, atop the dune that faces the sea, is a line of vegetation holding the island together with its roots, protecting the salt marsh behind, at least until a really big storm happens to hit this section of coast directly. When it comes, as it surely will, everything will change radically, at least for a few hundred years, until the river to the north deposits another bar and the struggling plants again establish their outpost at the edge of the sea.

For me there is no struggle, on this day at least; I'm running for fun, with my speed determined by the surface of the ground and by what feels good. The clouds scud by, the beach turns wider and flatter with occasional pools behind the first line of dunes, and the shells lying in the sand change in size and type. The island behind the high-water mark of the winter storms is wider here, and stands of trees are visible through the lower saddles in the rise of sand. The plants have managed to secrete some real soil back there, temporarily out of reach of the salt water.

Despite the glorious day, there aren't very many people about. Except where the road gives close access to the beach, few bother to walk far, and I have seen no one on the last three or four miles of sand. The birds and an occasional crab still hold the beach, though within a few months the summer crowds may penetrate even this portion of it.

Running on the beach gives an elemental joy, a sublime feeling of unity with the natural world that is rarely equaled.

As I near the other end of the island, people reappear in small numbers, for the tip can be reached by a road that runs along the other side of the dunes, beside the salt marshes. The beach flattens out even more near the mouth of the river that borders the island on the south, and I run through pools, the bottoms of which are sculpted into undulant forms. I concentrate on the footing to avoid turning an ankle, separated temporarily from my communion with the larger surroundings. I wonder whether I would have noticed the corrugations of the pool bottoms quite so much at the beginning of the run; fatigue may be beginning to show.

The beach curves around the end of the island. There are more rocks here, and a couple of stone jetties sweep out into the stretch of water where the river joins the sea. I check my watch, for I have to be back this afternoon, and I have been pushing the time a little because I wanted to go all the way to the end. I toy with the idea of running back on the road; it would be faster and different, but I would have to put up with the cars and would have no time to explore any of the side trails through the trees or into the marsh. Besides, I'm not ready to break off my contact with the beach and the ocean just yet. I turn and run back through the pools again, soon reaching the more enjoyable running on the hard sand at the edge of the water. The tide is higher by now, so the route has changed a bit. I'm also running into the gusty wind now. It slows me and whips the sand around, enough to fill my hair with fine grains but not so hard as to be unpleasant. The tree swallows swooping along the beach catching insects make use of each gust, twisting and turning with seemingly effortless grace. My running gives me just enough of a taste of the physical pleasure of that movement to feel a kinship with the birds, but by comparison I am clumsy and straining. A gull hangs up ahead in an equally enviable pose, balancing just above the breakers on the crest of a wave of air, tilting the leading edges of the wings ever so slightly to adjust to the changing currents, the essence of precise control.

I think with some trepidation about the stretches of soft sand ahead on the way back. I have less energy to spare now. As I start sinking into the first such area, my zigzagging in search of harder ground to no avail, I can feel the abrasion of the sharp grains of sand. I may have to put on my shoes yet. As the miles add up, even soft sand begins to make its grittiness felt. Neither the friction nor the effort is as bad as I thought it might be, though, and I manage to keep up my pace through the soft section, breathing a bit harder but not really tired. I stop worrying about the time and watch the magic water, rolling on forever to the east.

The Running Habit

We are creatures of habit through most of our daily lives, a trait more often positive than negative. We get through most of our normal chores by habit. One of the reasons it is hard to get started running is that to do so, you have to break some old habits and establish a new set for part of the day. The key to all the positive aspects of running is regularity. You have to run as part of your normal routine to make progress and to enjoy the activity. Hard running on infrequent occasions has little beneficial training effect, can often cause injuries, and does not help to establish the routine the beginner has to set as a first priority.

One of the things you can look forward to during the first few months of running—the hard ones—is the establishment of running as a regular habit. If you run in the morning, it will be desperately hard at first if you are like most people, because you have to make a decision to get out of bed and get going when the alarm goes off. As the run becomes established as something you *do* every morning, rather than something you *decide* to do, getting out will become progressively easier. All this has nothing to do with enjoyment; ten minutes after I get up in the morning I am en-joying my run, but those first dank minutes I manage by habit.

Running is habit forming in other senses as well. It becomes an important part of the life of most regular runners, serving to fill many physical and emotional needs: giving a sense of bodily well-being, relieving tension in the muscles and the mind, and provid-ing a time to think (or not think). Runners who miss their daily runs tend to feel the lack rather strongly.

For some, running is physically addictive. Deprived of their daily runs, many runners are ill at ease, have a hard time getting to sleep, or are irritable, anxious, and depressed. Not all regular run-ners experience these withdrawal problems when they are forced to stop running for a while, but the fact that many do indicates how important regular running can become. Clearly, when running becomes this firmly established as a part of one's life and daily rou-tine, it is not too difficult to maintain the habit of running regu-larly.

The most important step in getting into the habit is finding and deciding on a time or set of times when you can manage to run every day. I have come to enjoy running in the early morning, but the main reason I started running at that time is that it is the only time when I can nearly always manage to go. The rest of my days and evenings are busy enough and variable enough that I am likely to end up missing my run if I rely on going at some other time. There is no good excuse for not getting out in the morning; if I don't do it, the problem is sheer laziness.

In setting up a schedule for yourself, it is important to be real-istic and to set specific times that you can hold yourself to. It is no good setting the morning as your time unless you can get to bed in time to wake up for the morning run nor to settle on lunchtime if you frequently have to have business lunch meetings. On the other hand, no one is really so busy that the time cannot be set aside at some part of the day if he or she is serious about running regularly.

Lunch break is often a good time to run. Many people have a long enough break then with no important commitments. Skipping lunch helps control weight, and a run at that time usually sup-presses hunger quite effectively once one is used to the exercise. Until you are accustomed to it, a light, quick snack while you are getting dressed will do nicely, and it will probably have a lot fewer calories than you would consume if you spent the whole period at lunch. The main problem to be overcome for most people who work is a spot to change and shower.

A lot of runners manage without a shower, maintaining that the perspiration caused by moderate exercise is usually odorless. This is definitely not the case if you are losing weight, however, as many beginners are likely to be. No polls have been taken among the coworkers of showerless runners either, and I have my doubts that the odorless verdict is unanimous. Personally, I feel uncomfortable unless I have my shower after a run, so running at noon would depend on the availability of a shower for me. It is often possible with a little diligence to find one nearby and to get permission to use it. Many companies can be persuaded to install one if they are lobbied extensively with emphasis on the benefits of good employee health. YMCAs, YWCAs, city gyms, and the like all are possible locations if one is nearby. Women should not tolerate lack of access if there are showers for men. If a women's shower is not available and is financially impractical, times to share facilities can easily be scheduled.

If morning or the noon hour is not convenient for you, try to block out a time in the afternoon or evening. Before supper is a good time if you can manage it, because the run tends to reduce appetite. After a meal it is usually best to wait at least a couple of hours unless it is a light one, so if you pick a time after supper, allow time to digest your food.

Try to set aside an hour or so for your running from the time you begin. You may modify the length of the workout later, but you need at least this much time to get the endurance exercise that is important in a daily workout. The reasons for starting with long periods from the very beginning will be discussed in more detail later, but the point is to stress the body easily over a period of time rather than strain it with short-term hard work. You need a few minutes to change clothes and stretch before you start, several minutes of easy effort to warm up at the beginning of your run (particularly early in the morning), and time to stretch, shower, and change when you are done. Thus, even an hour gives you only forty-five minutes or less for your actual running.

Blocking out enough time also allows you to maintain your habits for a reasonable length of time without having to shift things once again after a few weeks, when your capacity begins to increase. Remember that establishing the habit of regular running is the most important goal to achieve in the first six months. Conditioning, weight loss, and faster times will all come easily and without real extra effort if you can manage to get into the habit of running.

A number of other factors may be important in beginning to run regularly. It is a great help to many people to have someone else to run with, perhaps for company or just to provide the extra incentive that may be needed to get out on the difficult days when willpower is at an ebb. Personally, I find that when I am running in the morning, it is a big help to know that someone else is waiting out in the cold, predawn light on those mornings when my body does not want to rise; at other times of day, it doesn't matter much to me whether I have company or not. Some runners like to go out with others a few times a week but alone most days. If you do run with someone else, be reliable and make the running dates you set; it will help keep the momentum going for both of you. Try to find someone who is well motivated, so that he or she will help you keep going rather than giving you an excuse to miss days. If your companion does slack off, don't let that become an excuse for stopping yourself. You might have to try several people before things work out. Good running partners may be hard to find.

Developing the running habit is one of the important arguments in favor of trying to run every day, or at least five days a week. Of course, you will miss some days, but by assuming that you will run *every* day, skipping days only when it is unavoidable, regularity is established so that you don't have to make an effort to get out on most occasions. Some experts argue that for fitness, running three days a week is enough to produce the desired conditioning effect, although this contention is debatable. More important is that it becomes very difficult to maintain a running schedule every other day. Most people either make running a daily routine or eventually drop it.

In establishing a regular running routine, you will probably have to juggle your schedule and make some changes in other aspects of your life. Most people who become runners are already busy and don't have large blocks of time during the day when they have nothing to do. Like most really worthwhile things, running does demand a certain amount of sacrifice and dedication. It is important to recognize this when you start, or you will find that you never have the time to run. Later on, you are likely to find that running really doesn't take away from the rest of your life. You will feel better, have more stamina, and be better able to concentrate on your other activities. At the beginning, though, making a real mental commitment to putting some of your time and energy into your running program is the best way to be sure of success.

Walking, Jogging, and Running

There is a lot of overlapping between walking, jogging, and running; in fact, the words have different meanings and connotations to different people. A serious race walker can walk faster than most people can run. A pace that is flat-out running for me would probably be considered an easy jogging rate to champion marathoner Frank Shorter. To some the difference between jogging and running is one of speed, to others a matter of form and stride, and to still others it is a distinction in mental cast and attitude.

From a technical point of view, there are strict definitions of walking that apply to racers: one foot has to be in contact with the

Regularity is the key to both enjoyment of running and the physical conditioning it can provide. Finding a place where you enjoy running will help you establish the habit.

1976 AAU cross-country champion Rick Rojas is one of the country's top distance runners.

ground at all times, and the leg pushing the body forward has to be straight by the time the body passes over it. On the other hand, in terms of demands on the body and the training required, the pace of eight minutes per mile over twenty kilometers (twelve and a half miles) that may be achieved by race walkers is a world apart from what most people mean by *walking*. A lot of runners have to work for a long time before they can achieve an eight-minutes-per-mile pace over long distances.

Walking, jogging, and running represent a progression that most people who are starting out should follow. With few exceptions, the beginning runner can no more go out and start running long distances than he or she could commence piano lessons by playing a Liszt concerto. Endurance is built from the foundations up, like a house, and impatience is likely to result in the edifice crumbling because the base is unsound. Most people should begin by alternately walking and jogging for some length of time each day, gradually picking up the tempo as they become more fit. Many need to start off with a walking program alone, walking a bit faster and farther as they acquire more stamina and slowly working into a walking and jogging routine. Running all out for a few hundred yards, only to collapse with the heart beating wildly and with breathing out of control for ten minutes, is an effort that does very little for endurance training, can be dangerous for people with weak hearts, and is unlikely to help establish the habit of regular exercise. Move up to running tempos slowly and steadily and you will be far more likely to achieve the rewards they can bring.

Experienced runners generally follow this same routine in miniature every day. The body does not spring willingly into extreme effort. The muscles need to be warmed up, stretched, and loosened before having maximum demands placed on them. The runner normally starts off with some slow warm-up routine before trying to run hard, particularly if he or she is running right after getting up in the morning. Typically, after a little stretching and walking, the morning run begins with an easy jog and the pace picks up gradually. Too fast a start always risks injury, whether you are starting your first run or your thousandth.

A *Philosophy of Running*

The unity between mind and body is one of the discoveries you will make again and again in your daily running, but it is not a perception that can be cheaply or quickly won. Americans are an impatient people, and they tend to search for the quick and easy way to a goal. The physical and mental rewards that can be achieved by running can't be had this way. They must be approached slowly and steadily. It's impossible to get into shape in a few months or to stay in condition on a few minutes of exercise every other day. It's harmful to race too many times in a single year. Moreover, the greatest rewards of running are generally perceived along the way. Running a particular race or achieving a particular level of fitness is satisfying, but the best experiences are often the gratuitous ones: running along among the spring flowers at sunrise or feeling a burst of energy under a crackling cold winter sky. You'll have your share of these rewards in your tenth month and your tenth year of running. Pace yourself for the long haul, for the runs that you want to take when you're sixty or seventy years old. The rest will take care of itself.

2/ *Beginnings*

The single most important action for the beginning runner to take is to go out and run! This is an easy point to lose sight of in the midst of cautioning people to avoid overstress. You may or may not decide that you need a physical examination before you start running, but the overall risks of maintaining a sedentary life are far greater than the chance of being hurt by exercise. Authors and physicians sometimes misplace their emphasis on the conservative side as they envision some reader or patient ripe for a heart attack going out on a hot day in midsummer and running himself to exhaustion. As long as you maintain a little common sense, the risks involved with starting a running program are minimal and the rewards are great.

This chapter begins by discussing the advantages and limitations of physical examinations. Some recommendations are included on the kind of physical you need if you decide that an exam is advisable for you. Preliminaries aside, you need to develop a realistic notion of your starting point—the physical condition you are in now. Such an evaluation is considered in detail, and recommendations follow on what kind of running or walking program you should use to begin and on what initial goals you should set for yourself. Finally, the chapter goes into schedules, places to run, and similar matters.

Through all this discussion, try to keep your main objectives in mind. Get out and make your muscles work a little. Even if you start with just a vigorous walk around the park, make a beginning and then keep it up.

Do You Need a Physical Examination?

This is a question that is at the center of much controversy both in and out of the medical profession, and it is not easy to answer because there are so many factors involved. If you are young, physically active, and have no reason to worry about your health, you don't need a physical. You don't need a doctor to tell you that you feel well. If, on the other hand, you are an older person, have lived a sedentary life for a number of years, and have a number of high-risk factors for a heart attack, it is prudent to have a thorough physical examination before engaging in really strenuous exercise. Specific factors that increase the risk of heart attack are a history of heart or circulatory ailments in your family, obesity, high blood pressure, smoking, a tense personality or a style of life that puts you under frequent stress, being a male, and diabetes. Other factors that may have been diagnosed by your physician in the past should also be taken into account. You should make a particular point of having a physical (unless you are already physically very active) if you have any specific health problems, if you are over fifty, if you are over forty and have two or three of the risk factors mentioned, or if you are over thirty-five and have a number of them.

Most of us know whether we are basically healthy or not if we are honest with ourselves, and it makes sense to have a physical examination before you start a serious running program if you have doubts about your health. Even if you are quite well, uncertainty about the safety of running is a good enough reason to be checked by a doctor, if only to put your own mind at ease, so that you won't have lingering anxieties when you go out the door to run.

We have gotten so used to an inactive and unhealthy life as the norm that moderate exercise has come to be regarded as an unusual activity. We assume that we require clearance from a panel of experts before engaging in it. Unfortunately, this attitude all too often means that people never get around to exercising at all. Instead of running around the block one morning when the impulse strikes, they put off running until after a physical exam that is scheduled six weeks hence, after they've had a chance to purchase the proper equipment, and after a host of other obstacles. The habit they establish is *putting off* running every day.

There are several objections that many runners have to physical examinations as a stock prescription. Recently, somewhat similar objections have been voiced within the medical profession. Most such objections arise from two basic problems: first, the average physical is expensive but not very thorough, and second, most doctors are disease oriented, consider sedentary, overweight, out-of-shape people to be the "healthy" norm, and are completely unfamiliar with the characteristics of the fit, athletic individual.

The first objection is the one raised by those members of the medical profession who are dissatisfied with the standard once-a-year physical. It is also the one that most frequently applies to beginning runners. My own opinion is that if you are young, healthy, and reasonably active, the physical is probably unnecessary. If you are middle-aged, have been sedentary for some time, or have other risk factors, you should have a physical. I would include the proviso, however, that the standard once-over-lightly examination is fairly worthless for detecting the conditions that would cause problems if you start running. If you're going to have a physical exam, then it ought to be a thorough one with a stress test (see below) that brings your heart up fairly close to maximum output (assuming you haven't already detected heart disease). This is important because incipient problems are more likely to be detected at that level. A good physical of this type will detect most diseases that might require modification of a running plan. You must also exercise your own good judgment in deciding what shape you're in, to decide on whether you need an examination and how to start your program.

Most of us place far too much reliance on technology to interpret the world and even ourselves. We forget simpler and sometimes more accurate sources of information. The runner has to learn to pay attention to signals from the body. The way you feel from day to day and during a run is the best single indicator of your state of health and of the effects of training, illness, and so on. The more sensitive you become to those signals, the more accurate your understanding will be of what is going on in your body. The purpose of medical instruments and technology is to supplement that understanding, not to replace it.

When a middle-aged, overweight smoker with a high-pressure desk job drops dead from a heart attack while shoveling his sidewalk, we blame his death on the snowstorm, though a little thought will tell us that the effort would have caused him no difficulty had he weighed thirty pounds less, gotten some exercise every day, stopped smoking, and found a way to relieve the tensions of his work. Similarly, the typical person who has a heart attack while running is middle-aged and overweight, hasn't engaged in any activity for years, and starts running as though pursued by hungry wolves. Be warned: if you have heart disease, you may die running; you may also die while going to the bathroom (quite common), eating, sleeping in your bed, or having a physical exam. No warranty of immortality is available, at least from secular sources.

The unfamiliarity of the average doctor with the normal body of a trained athlete tends to be more of a problem for regular runners than for beginners, though former athletes who are getting back into things should beware. Distance runners and other endurance athletes in particular exhibit characteristics that are perfectly healthy but may alarm the average doctor. Individuals in this category might want to make a particular effort to find a doctor familiar with runners to do their examinations.

For most people, the results of a physical examination will simply be a conclusion that nothing is wrong that would preclude a vigorous exercise program. (You should still avoid overstressing yourself, particularly in the first few weeks as your body begins to adapt.) Those people showing some signs of heart disease will of course have to approach running slowly and with caution, with advice from a physician. Usually they should begin with walking for progressively increasing distances. There are programs in many areas for cardiac patients, and there are certainly advantages in participating in group programs if you do have heart disease. The medical personnel involved with such programs are knowledgeable both in exercise physiology and in cardiac care. Many such programs are conducted in association with the YMCA, so the local Y is a good place to call for information on whether such a group exists where you live.

One other point is worth making here. With only a modicum of common sense, anyone can develop a sensitivity to the amount of stress involved in exercising and adjust the level along the way.

High-intensity trials of strength, such as lifting heavy weights or doing isometric exercises, tend to make the blood pressure soar rapidly, but endurance exercises place gradual stress on the system—stress that you monitor, whether you like it or not. As long as the intensity of such exercise is increased gradually, your pulse rate, breathing, and perspiration will tell you how hard you're working. One of the obvious precautions you should take if you are seriously out of shape is to keep the effort moderate at the beginning, increasing it gradually as your condition and tolerance improve.

What Kind of Physical Examination?

The single most important medical test for someone beginning a running program is a stress electrocardiogram. An electrocardiogram is a graphed recording of the electrical activity of the heart, which can be closely correlated with its function. Most electrocardiograms are taken while the patient is at rest, so they don't show the way the heart functions during strenuous exertion and the subsequent recovery period. The stress electrocardiogram, taken while the subject is working at various levels of effort, is far more likely to reveal heart disease and to enable a physician to advise a patient on what sort of exercise to start with. Most commonly, a stress electrocardiogram is taken while the subject exercises on a treadmill or a stationary bicycle with calibrated resistance, but any standard exercise bicycle with graduated resistance can be used; so can a high step. The requirement for this purpose is simply a continuous, adjustable level of effort so that the heart can be induced to pump at increasing pulse rates up to its capacity. If possible it is advisable to have the stress test done by a doctor who is a runner or at least one familiar with the sport and sympathetic to it. Such a physician will be better able to advise a would-be runner and will be more familiar with the stresses one will undergo.

Doctors who are runners themselves (and there are many of them) can be very helpful in giving you advice on how to start running and how to avoid overstress. They are also much more likely to have an accurate idea of the physiology of running than an overweight doctor who smokes and regards jogging as a crazy fad.

A sympathetic and knowledgeable physician can be very important for a runner, particularly a novice, whereas a doctor who does not believe in strenuous exercise can be deeply discouraging. Hundreds of runners have had the unpleasant experience of being told by an ill-informed physician that they have pathological heart irregularities and should avoid all strenuous exercise, only to find out later that there was nothing wrong with them. Clarence DeMar, one of the greatest American marathon runners of the past, had an extremely strong and healthy heart, as an autopsy proved after his death from cancer, yet he missed the best years of his career because he was mistakenly told by a doctor that he suffered from heart disease and should not run. After a number of years, he finally disregarded the advice, returning to championship running and demonstrating the error of the diagnosis.

Another example of a mistaken idea about strenuous exercise is that for years it was a common belief in the medical profession that the enlargement of the muscle mass of the heart, or "athlete's heart," which is common in distance runners and other endurance athletes, posed a severe danger to health in later years, making the possessor of such a curse prone to heart attacks and all manner of ailments. In fact, this is nonsense and, if anything, is the reverse of the truth. Victims of high blood pressure and some kinds of heart disease do have enlarged hearts, but the enlargement is not caused by exercise. This strange old doctor's tale probably has its origin in the tendency of some high school and college athletes to maintain their adolescent eating habits as they move into a less active middle age and to develop the tendency toward heart disease that is characteristic of obesity. The result of the error, however, was to discourage exercise on the ground that the practitioner might acquire athlete's heart.

It is important that we start thinking in a balanced way about the stresses we place on our bodies and begin to understand that physical work in the fresh air is not a dubious risk but rather a necessary function for good health, one for which our bodies were designed by millions of years of evolution, which we frustrate at our peril. This is even more true for the individual who has reason to fear diseases of the heart and circulatory system, since endurance exercise can assist in controlling many of the factors that increase the risk of such disorders.

What Kind of Shape Are You In?

A reasonable analysis of your own physical condition is the first step in planning any kind of exercise program, including a running program, whether or not you see a doctor for a physical examination as well. It is important to evaluate your own health and level of fitness as accurately as possible in order to maintain a reasonable margin of safety and to set realistic goals for yourself in the immediate future. You want to have objectives that are hard enough to give you something to work toward but easy enough to be attainable, and you want to avoid injuring yourself in trying to reach your goals. After such an assessment you'll be better able to decide whether you need a physical exam and to evaluate what the doctor tells you if you have one.

Vanity can be a real impediment to evaluating your physical condition, although it may also be one of the best reservoirs of motivation for conditioning. Most people don't like to think about what bad shape they are in, compared with what they could be. It seems to be human nature to avoid confronting this sort of issue by one rationalization or another. Think about what you are doing positively and you may be able to avoid this trap. Remember that the function of a self-examination is to decide how best to improve your level of fitness safely. One of the positive aspects of being in really poor condition (provided you haven't developed serious health problems as a result) is that you can make a lot of progress with relatively little effort. The average person can develop far more endurance, feel much better, and get a lot of satisfaction with thirty minutes' work a day. An Olympic athlete has to spend many hours each day just for incremental improvements.

The marathon provides a convenient standard by which to gauge your potential. The race was named for the legendary run made by a soldier from the plains of Marathon to the city of Athens to bring the news of the victory over the Persians. The distance of the marathon (26 miles, 385 yards) seems incredible to most beginning runners, quite beyond the capacity of normal people. On the contrary, marathons are run every year by thousands of men, women, and children who have no extraordinary talent or physical endowments. Kevin Strain at the age of five ran one a little faster than Claude Mulholland when the latter was eighty-four. Bob Hall, a polio victim, pushes his wheelchair over a marathon course faster than most runners can move their legs the same distance. Many former victims of heart attack, using carefully graduated training runs as therapy, have eventually advanced to the marathon, a powerful demonstration of their achievement of a better state of health than they enjoyed before their attacks. Probably any healthy individual without a handicap of extreme age or disability can train to run a marathon in creditable time.

Age is not even a significant disability, except for toddlers or those who have already gotten past their allotted three score and ten. Although maximum potential performance does slowly decline with age, much of the decline can be postponed with training. Age-related decreases in capacity also affect the endurance athlete far more slowly than the sprinter or high jumper. Amazingly, this is true even at the level of world-class competition. Jack Foster, a great New Zealand distance runner, didn't even start running until he was in his thirties. When he was nearly forty-two, he ran the marathon in 2:11:18, less than three minutes over the world record. Miki Gorman was the woman winner at Boston in 1974, New York in 1976, and again at Boston in 1977, when she was forty-one. She too started running in her thirties, so most of the rest of us can't use our age as an excuse.

Although few people are likely to join the ranks of world-class competitors, running distances at more modest speeds is within the capacity of nearly everyone willing to work a little each day. But you cannot expect to undo twenty years of diligent loafing in a few months. Progress generally comes slowly, particularly if you want to avoid injury.

Age is a factor to consider, however. Its most important influence is on the resilience of the body in response to training stresses. If you are fifty, you can't expect to get into good condition as quickly as you might have at twenty-five. This is no reason to be discouraged, however, because ultimately you can achieve results that are almost as good. In fact, allowing for the reduced expectations that most people seem to have of their physical capacity as they get older, the fifty-year-old can expect much better results. A difference of a few minutes in potential race times is inconsequential. The good news is that you can easily surpass the physical con-

Few of us are in condition to begin running hard for any distance. A realistic view of your own condition is important to help establish goals for the first few months.

dition of the great majority of people in their twenties. In terms of training schedules and short-term goals, however, the older person has to expect to start at a lower level of stress than the younger one and to progress at a more moderate rate.

Your weight is critical in almost every respect. The more extra pounds you are carrying, the more work your heart has to do just to supply the tissues with an adequate blood flow. Excess fat is a factor in most degenerative diseases, particularly those of the circulatory system. In any exercise that involves lifting the body, including running, extra weight imposes a particular disability because it places an extra load on the whole system. There is no need to go into a detailed analysis of weight and fat content here. Much of the body's fat is carried just under the skin, particularly around the abdomen, hips, thighs, and upper arms. If you are very much overweight, you are certainly aware of it; if you have a significant "spare tire," or roll of fat around your middle, then you are carrying a lot of extra weight. For those who are a little leaner, there are two quick indications that can be used: (1) Any weight you have gained since the age of about eighteen is fat, unless you have engaged extensively in some kind of body-building exercise like heavy weight lifting, which can add a lot of muscle mass. (2) Pinch out a skin fold on the back of your hand to feel how thick it is. Now do the same thing in the fleshy areas just above your hip bones, at the abdomen a few inches to one side of your navel, on your back below a shoulder blade, and on the back of your upper arm a few inches below the armpit, with the muscle tensed. All that extra thickness you feel beyond what you felt on the back of the hand is stored fat. It is dead weight, and the more you have, the more unnecessary a burden there is on the rest of the system. The average American overeats, and even those of us who would not be considered overweight by most of our acquaintances are usually carrying around about 25 percent more weight than we need.

The amount of exercise you can undertake at the beginning will be determined in large measure by the level of activity you're used to. If you regularly engage in work or recreation that requires sustained physical effort, you will obviously be able to run farther and faster than if you've gotten very little exercise in the last few years. Evaluating your activity level is bound to be subjective, like most of the items mentioned here, but it is important to be realistic. Even if you carry your own clubs, golf is a fairly mild activity. Tennis, though it can be a strenuous game when played by skilled players, involves only a moderate amount of activity in the average doubles game. On the other hand, if you regularly engage in rigorous games of soccer, squash, fast-paced tennis, and the like, you'll be able to start a running program at a much higher level.

The scoring system in the chart on pages 34–35 is intended to help you estimate your own level of conditioning. It isn't precise and doesn't really need to be, because its purpose is simply to help you decide how hard to work when you start running and to give you an idea of what to expect. Remember that there aren't any prizes for a low score, especially if you deceive yourself and try to go too hard at the beginning.

Beginning Programs

Use your score from the chart on pages 34–35 to get started. The list below should give a rough guide to the level at which you should begin. If you find yourself puffing uncontrollably or becoming exhausted, slow down. If you complete forty-five minutes or an hour without even feeling pressed, go up a level the next day. Do not try to push too fast, and once you have found the proper starting level, let your body tell you how to proceed.

NUMBER OF POINTS	STARTING LEVEL
Less than 10	Begin by alternately running easily and slowing to a very easy jog whenever you start to get winded. Keep yourself working, but if you become winded or really tired, walk for a few hundred yards and drop to jogging rather than running.
10–15	Begin by jogging and walking alternately. Try to keep the walks brisk. Begin jogging as soon as you feel well rested, and taper off to a walk as soon as you get winded or become tired.
16–20	Begin by walking briskly. Walk at a good pace the whole way the first two days. If this is not too hard, jog for a block occasionally during the walk. Gradually increase the proportion of jogging.
21–25	Walk briskly, and when you begin to get winded, slow down to a more comfortable pace. Learn to pace yourself so that after your workout you feel pleasantly tired but bounce back rapidly. Increase the pace until you can walk for the whole period briskly, then begin to introduce jogging intervals.
Over 25	Walk for forty-five minutes to an hour, increasing the pace to a brisk walk whenever you feel you're just strolling along and slowing again when you feel winded. Progress as your body dictates.

POINTS	0	1	2	
AGE	20 or younger	21–30	31–40	
ACTIVITY LEVEL	Always very active, including regular endurance work, such as competitive sports involving constant motion for extended periods, frequent vigorous hiking, mountaineering, extensive bicycling, swimming steadily for more than 30 minutes, on an average of 2 or 3 days a week.	Similarly active on an average of a day or two a week, and also engage in frequent walking, cycling, and active sports or work such as most tennis, softball, energetic dancing, manual labor, etc.	Engage regularly at least three times a week in activities involving some running, lengthy walking, bicycling at least 30 minutes at a time, swimming, or similar physical work.	
FAT LEVEL	No excess fat. Many people consider you to be much too skinny and tell you to eat more and put some meat on your bones. Pinch test finds no telltale folds.	Very slim and lean by normal standards. Most people would describe you as thin. Pinch test finds a little fatty tissue around your waist, but only small amounts.	Trim and fit with no extra fat by conventional standards. Face, legs, arms, and stomach have no little bulges of fat. ½" pinch at waist for men and ¾" for women.	
GENERAL HEALTH	Perfect health. Always feel well and are rarely ill. Always have plenty of bounce and energy through the day.	Try to rate yourself honestly between these extremes. Those with identifiable illnesses should consult a physician.		
SMOKING	Never smoked. Do not work or live in an area that is frequently filled with smoke by others.	Live or work in a place where you often get a dose of other people's smoke. Former smoker who quit more than 2 years ago.	Former smoker who quit more than a year ago.	
RESTING PULSE (Take in morning before rising.)	Under 50	51–60	61–70	

NOTE: This chart is intended to serve as a gauge for people who would generally be considered to be in a normal state of health. If you are diabetic, have suffered from a heart attack or been diagnosed as having heart disease, have high blood pressure, are a smoker starting to show signs

3	4	5
41–50	51–60	Over 60
Occasionally participate in activities that demand strenuous work for some time and often take walks, bike rides, etc., or work at a job that requires some regular physical stress.	Walk farther than to and from the car, dance, or do some work involving the body's large muscles fairly regularly; more active until a couple of years ago.	Have engaged in little vigorous physical activity for several years.
Average build that would not generally be considered at all over-weight. No paunch or spare tire, but enough extra flesh in your middle to get a handful.	Have what would normally be considered to be a little extra weight. A bit of a paunch or spare tire in the middle, but not enough to interfere at all with normal physical activity.	Chubby. Anyone fatter, unless they are accustomed to regular strenuous exercise, should start with a diet and a walking program.
Try to rate yourself honestly between these extremes. Those with identifiable illnesses should consult a physician.		Don't feel very well these days, but have no serious illness or problem a doctor can pin down.
Former smoker who quit more than six months ago.	Cigarette smokers who smoke less than a pack a day, cigar and pipe smokers who do not inhale, and those who've quit within six months.	Cigarette smokers who smoke a pack or more a day and pipe and cigar smokers who inhale.
71–80	81–90	Over 90; should be checked by physician unless you've had this rate for a while and have been checked before.

of lung disease, or have any other serious illness, it is only prudent to start your running program under the supervision of a doctor.

Basics

At higher levels of conditioning there is a lot of disagreement about training methods. For the beginning runner, however, the best way to start is by covering a lot of distance at a relatively low speed. You want to go fast enough to make your body work without hurting yourself. If you try to start off at the rate that an experienced runner would travel, you'll probably have to stop, panting and puffing, before you've made your heart and lungs work long enough to do them much good. At the same time, you'll probably end up with a lot of aches and pains that will interfere with the next day's workout. A longer, slower session will start to condition your legs and the rest of your body to the movements and duration of a long run, toughen your feet, and get the blood pumping around in your body long enough to start to condition your heart and circulatory system.

The rule of thumb you should observe, especially for your first few weeks of training, is to move along as fast as you can without having to breathe hard. Regulate your effort so that you can carry on a normal conversation with your running companion, hum a little song to yourself, or whatever. You should be breathing a little more deeply and rapidly than usual, but if you have to gasp out phrases or sentences when you are talking, slow down a little. The pace at which you can breathe comfortably may range from a walk or a slow jog to a quick run, depending on your condition, but for the beginner it will usually be quite slow. The older you are or the more out of shape you are, the more careful you should be not to exert yourself to the point of breathlessness.

Keep in mind that it is endurance strength and cardiopulmonary conditioning that you really need, not speed. Most people can take off running very rapidly indeed; what they can't do is to maintain that speed for any length of time. The best way to build up endurance is to go at a moderate speed for some length of time, even if that speed amounts to a brisk walk. Don't let the seemingly slow pace discourage you. As long as you are moving fast enough to induce deep, strong breathing (but not panting) and to make you sweat after you've been moving for a while, your endurance and speed will start to improve.

The object of each day's workout should be to cover as much ground as you can in forty-five minutes or an hour without becoming exhausted or badly out of breath. At the end of your walk, jog, or run, you should feel pleasantly tired, but you should revive by the time you've showered and dressed. If the aftereffects are more pronounced than that, let up somewhat the next day. Excessive fatigue is a sign that you've pushed your body too far, draining your reserves of energy. You want to stimulate your system to strengthen itself, but pushing it too far will require a lot of energy to be spent replenishing your basic strength instead of building new endurance. If, on the other hand, you come back from your workout feeling as though you've scarcely started, work harder the following day; you haven't pushed your body enough to stimulate it to strengthen itself. After a couple of days you'll develop a pretty accurate idea of the pace that is right for you to get a workout without straining yourself. Listen to your body. It will tell you everything you need to know about proper pacing, provided you pay attention.

If you find that you're making a substantial effort to keep your pace for the full length of the workout, don't try to push yourself any harder for a while. Depending on your own body, it may take a few weeks or even a couple of months before you start to notice improvement. Be sensitive to signs that you are overdoing things: persistent fatigue, irritability, difficulty in getting to sleep or need for excessive amounts of sleep, and aches and pains, particularly those that don't go away and get worse during a workout. (More detailed information on overstress will be given later.)

Once the workouts start to feel comfortable and well within your capacity, start to experiment a little with pace. Alternate jogging and faster running at various speeds and intervals. Mix things up a little. Try running a few easy hills. Stride out occasionally, and play with your technique. Try picking your knees up and putting a little more vigor in your arm motion. Try to run so that your feet land very gently. See what happens when you move your legs faster in shorter strides. Playing with your pace and technique this way will teach you a lot about running style and make your runs more enjoyable. Start to have fun. Remember to keep your basic pace at a level that doesn't make you work too hard, however. Endurance is still the main object.

The suggestions that follow are based on a forty-five-minute time block, which allows enough time for stretching and a quick shower within a total of an hour. The time and distance can be adjusted in either direction to fit in with your own schedule, but three-quarters of an hour of actual exercise is a good period to start with. You can make a lot of progress using this schedule without having to change it every few weeks.

If you've estimated your condition from the chart, start off at the level suggested for a few days unless it feels very hard. *Don't push yourself yet.* Drop down to a lower speed and a lower level of stress if you find yourself panting or getting very tired. Later on, as your body becomes better conditioned, you will be able to run at top speed, again and again, and your system will bounce right back after a few minutes of walking or jogging. At the beginning, however, you will just risk tearing a muscle or having a heart attack if you push your body beyond its limits.

If you decide just to start off without estimating your condition, begin by walking for at least a week, gradually increasing the rate until you find a pace you can maintain for forty-five minutes that keeps you breathing more deeply and rapidly than you would at rest but doesn't make you lose your breath. If you start at a level suggested by the chart, you should adjust your pace during the first few days to reach that same level of exertion. To begin:

1. The pace (or the combination of slow and fast paces) should be fairly even for the entire forty-five minutes. If you tire and slow down partway through, you are starting too fast. Hills will naturally slow you down, but you should recover quickly at the top.

2. You should never get completely out of breath. If you are starting with a combination of walking and jogging or jogging and running, you'll get a little winded during the fast periods, but you should recover quickly as soon as you slow down. If you're out of breath or don't recover quickly after a fast interval or a hill, you're going too fast. Walkers should never get out of breath at this stage of the game. Remember that you should be able to hold a conversation during your workout.

3. Take your pulse (see page 89) about ten minutes after

you've gotten back from your walk, jog, or run—perhaps after you shower. If it is over 100 beats a minute, you're working too hard. Go slower the next day.

4. Once you've found the pace that requires the right amount of exertion, plan to stick with it. Don't try to speed up until your workouts start to feel too easy. Make your increases gradual. On days when you don't feel as strong, slow down until the pace feels right. Don't strain.

5. Start slowly every day and pick up as you go along, rather than trying to start fast. This is especially important if you go out early in the morning. Your body needs a few minutes to loosen and warm up. You may want to begin with stretching exercises before a walk or run (see chapter 8). In any case, consider the first ten minutes of a workout to be a warming-up period, and don't try to push hard until your muscles have loosened.

6. If you are sick, don't run, but try not to miss a day unless you are sick. If you have a cold or the flu, skip your workout, or at least reduce its intensity. (For injuries, see chapter 9.) In general, unless you are sick or have a painful injury (minor stiffness doesn't count), ignore the complaints your body makes for the first ten minutes—they're just the excuses of a malingerer. If you don't feel well after the ten-minute warm-up, pay attention and either ease up or quit for the day.

Usually the best approach at the beginning is to start out and follow an interesting route for half the time you have allotted and then return by the same path or a parallel one. Circuits are nicer, but they are harder to plan until you know your pace fairly well. I have a few dozen loops of varying distance that I can run, starting from my house, depending on my mood, the weather, and the time available. The out-and-back course works well at the start, though, since it allows you to keep track easily of your pace from one day to the next. Furthermore, if you are on a tight schedule, you are assured that you won't run out of time while you are still a couple of miles from home. Of course, you can also use a local school track or make circuits of a convenient park, which may be a more pleasant setting than the roads or sidewalks.

Once you've found a good basic pace that you can maintain for three-quarters of an hour, you may want to measure the distance you're covering, to give yourself a basis to judge progress. On the other hand, since your real goal is personal improvement, you may find the best method is simply to keep going at the rate your body says is right, ignoring the numbers game for a time. In measuring your rate, it isn't necessary to be too precise, but you should try to get a figure that is accurate within a few tenths of a mile so that your basis of comparison is not misleading. If your normal route follows roads, you can simply measure it with your car's odometer. In using this method, it is a good idea to calibrate the odometer first, since errors of 20 percent are common. (Odometers commonly read high, giving an impression of higher gas mileage.) There are mile markers along highways in most parts of the country, placed there to allow drivers to check odometers; if you don't know where such a measured mile is located, call your state highway patrol or highway department and ask. Carefully note the beginning and ending readings over the measured course and you'll be able to calculate the number of miles indicated on your odometer for each mile covered on the ground. With this correction factor you should be able to get a good idea of the length of your course within a tenth of a mile or so. You could also find out your daily distance by going to a quarter-mile track at a local high school or college and walking or running around it at your regular pace for forty-five minutes.

A good rule of thumb would be to continue with a walking program alone until you can comfortably cover three miles in forty-five minutes. This is a pace that feels fairly brisk to the average person, and it is a good level to reach before you begin jogging. There are no hard-and-fast rules here, since some joggers move at a slower pace than this, whereas a good race walker can go twice this fast without breaking into a trot. Still, this distance is both a comfortable point at which to switch to a slow jog and an indication that your body is fit enough to make the transition to the greater stress of jogging and then running.

As you progress into mixed walking and jogging and then mixed jogging and running, try to keep your body in the same equilibrium that you did when walking. A little hard breathing is fine at this stage, but try to avoid getting completely out of breath.

Make the transitions gradual rather than going from a walk to a hard run. Speed up just a little so that the demand on your heart and lungs is just marginally greater. Maintain the faster pace for a while to see whether your breathing gradually gets harder, indicating that you are moving faster than your body can process the oxygen needed for a sustained pace. Before you are out of breath, slow down again. Gradually, the faster-paced intervals will last longer and longer, until you are covering the whole course at the new, accelerated rate. Then add some still faster intervals. In this way your pace will slowly increase over the weeks and months.

Where to Run

You can run almost anywhere. Try to find places that are enjoyable, stimulating, and aesthetically pleasing, but don't get too hung up in the search for an ideal place to run. If you have to work too hard just to get to a starting place, you're likely to end up using the difficulty as an excuse for missing workouts. Most people can start from their front door and find a variety of runs. As your distance increases, so will the possibilities available within a half-workout radius of your doorstep.

You don't need a track to run. In fact, despite its good surface and conveniently marked distance, I personally find the track to be a terrible place to run. It is a colossal bore to go around and around a uniform oval even on one day, let alone seven days a week. This is a matter of taste, and if there is a school track near you and you enjoy running there, by all means make use of it. You can also run in parks, along trails, over golf courses (at appropriate hours), on country roads, through business districts, or in residential neighborhoods. It's pleasant to vary the scenery, so why not run in all these places? The times when a particular spot is best are likely to vary anyway, so adjust your runs accordingly.

Much is made of different running surfaces, but it is usually not worth worrying too much about them. The ideal is a trail with a smooth surface that gives a little when the foot strikes it. An even grade covered with forest duff, pine needles, damp earth, or one of the artificial running surface mixtures is a dream come true, but rare. Grass is also a joy to run on if the ground is smooth or the grass very short. Golf courses are often good places to run early in

Unless you are already in excellent shape, start out by alternating jogging and walking, or simply walking at a brisk pace. Whether you use roads, sidewalks, a park, or a local high school track like this one, the important thing is to get out for forty-five minutes a day.

the morning or late at night, provided the groundskeepers don't try to discourage you. Grass can often conceal nasty holes, however, that can result in a turned ankle, especially when the ground below is dry and hard. Trails vary widely in quality from the runner's point of view, ranging from excellent surfaces to loose, rocky, treacherous ones. The latter have to be run with care and in good light to avoid injuries. In rural areas dirt roads may make for good running if there isn't too much traffic to raise dust and force the runner off the road. Gravel roads make good running when the texture of the gravel is fine but can be an abomination when covered with large, loose stones.

Most of the time, you will probably find yourself running on pavement, either on sidewalks or roads. Although it is a little jarring, this is not really so bad. Obstacles and holes are easy to see on pavement, even in poor light. You can run on pavement in almost any weather conditions—provided you can avoid being hit by cars. Aside from traffic hazards (discussed later), ice is the only weather-related condition that may stop you from running on roads. Pavement provides good traction and a regular surface that permits you to look around or go into a trance most of the time, rather than forcing you to watch your footing continually. The final advantage to pavement is, of course, that there is so much of it.

Running on roads and sidewalks will probably teach you a lot about your neighborhood and surroundings you never knew before. As your runs become longer, you can explore every unfenced route within a radius of ten miles. In the process, you'll probably find some really delightful spots you wouldn't have dreamed existed so close to home. This is all a dividend particularly welcome at the odd hours when many of us run. Even a big city shows a different face in the first light of dawn. Running through Chinatown in San Francisco as the shops are putting out their vegetables or along the wharves of Boston as the sun rises can be a special experience, if only to breathe the air before the cars get at it.

Barring possible safety problems from traffic or human assailants, you should rarely even have to put a lot of thought into the question of where to run. Just put on your old clothes and running shoes and head out the door. There is a world out there that automobile drivers never dream of. (The matter of safety from muggers can be a particular problem for women, so it is discussed, in chapter 6, but in some neighborhoods men may also have to give it some thought.)

Goals

The goals of your initial walks, jogs, or runs should be conservative. Psychologically, it's a lot better to set them too low and to be pleasantly surprised when you progress more rapidly than you anticipated than it is to have unrealistic expectations doomed to be frustrated. Keep in mind that your main purpose should be long-term health and conditioning, which is most effectively built up slowly. With proper pacing you can keep improving over a period of many years, particularly in terms of age-corrected performance. If you try to push too fast, however, you will burn out in a relatively short period.

The most important goal to set yourself is simply to keep going. Make a mental commitment to train regularly for three months without slacking off or judging your progress. Get out a minimum of five days a week. If you drop off for several days in a row, you'll have to regain lost ground. Actually running or walking every day for three months with few misses is the most important objective when you are starting out. Progress is tangible and guaranteed; as long as you get out for your forty-five minutes, you have met your obligation to yourself for the day. There are bound to be plateaus and setbacks in your conditioning from a day-to-day perspective, but over a three-month period you should be able to look back and see real change, more than enough to encourage you to go on after that.

Keeping a notebook to record your training is a good idea, provided you don't become too obsessed with numbers and times. Recording your resting pulse every month or so should give you one excellent indication of progress. A lower resting pulse means that major improvement is taking place. So will a note of the increased distance you are traveling in your daily workout. Try to avoid getting into a pattern of competing with yourself or your partner from one day to the next, however. You don't want to race anyone yet.

One object of the diary is to keep track of the regularity of your workouts. The number of days you skip will be right there in black and white so that an optimistic memory can't cheat. On a long-term basis the notes will show you how much progress you have made. This can be encouraging during periods when you don't seem to be improving at all. Later on, when you are running longer distances at a faster rate, the notebook will provide a good guide for training, giving you a record of the training schedules that have worked in the past and those that have failed.

In three months you should have made really significant progress, commensurate with your age and the level at which you began. If you are badly out of shape at the beginning, you won't become a competitive racer in three months, but you will make more progress than a person who started at a higher fitness level. The average middle-aged person will generally move from a poor walking pace to mixed jogging and running in that time. The person who started out with slow jogging will probably have progressed to an honest running pace over the whole distance. By the end of the three months you should be able to judge the effects of running on your health and fitness fairly accurately and be able to set long-term goals. This break-in period should also give you a good start at establishing regular running as a habit and an idea as to whether you are going to like it. Some people, perhaps those who are natural runners, will have already started really enjoying their daily runs by this time. Personally, I found that real pleasure in running itself came somewhat later, when I was in condition to do longer runs without having to beat myself into the ground just to finish. I did enjoy the feeling of fitness that I was getting from running, though, and the sense of progress one feels should be enough incentive to elicit another three-month commitment.

Competitive, hard-driving people should be particularly careful to try to keep compulsiveness and competition out of their running at this stage, for a number of reasons. Becoming competitive will make you want to work for speed much too soon, before you build up the endurance base that is essential to prevent injuries and to allow you to reach your potential in races. Racers even at top levels of competition frequently have this problem, and trying to raise the level of training before the body can withstand it is even more likely to bring the beginner to grief. The frustrations of injury and failure are quite likely to make the overenthusiastic novice racer quit running after a fairly short time, without ever having the experience of being in really good shape. Overtraining breaks the body down instead of building it up. Perhaps most important, emphasizing competition at the expense of other values at an early stage degrades both the running experience and the contributions it can make to one's life. The hard-driving person can gain particular benefits in relaxation of tension from running if, and only if, it does not become just one more place where the only object is to win.

Remember also that if you are in this group, the competitive drive can manifest itself in many ways. It isn't confined to racing or training for races. If you run with other people, run for companionship rather than in competition. Don't compete with yourself every time you go out, always trying to run a little faster or longer than the day before, to drive yourself a little harder. You will improve, but there will be off days as well as long periods dur-

Your long-term goal should be to achieve a state of fitness that will allow you to run at good speeds for long distances. You also need short-term objectives, however, commensurate with the shape you are in now.

ing which there is little improvement or even some deterioration. The body responds to stress over extended lengths of time. Many highly trained distance runners have found that an increase in their training load doesn't have any significant effect for six weeks. Be patient. If you are very compulsive, it might be better not to keep a running diary for a while, or at least to keep track only of the time *or* distance you ran, not both. This way you won't feel the need every day to try to better your performance. Even if you do get into racing, you can't go all out very often, particularly over long distances. Most runs should be done at a much slower pace to build up endurance, at least for your first few years of running.

A long-term goal may be useful once you've gotten far enough to see some progress and to realize that with enough perseverance you can do a lot more than you ever dreamed. Running a marathon is a common long-term goal, and it is a good one, because a lot of long training runs are required at moderate speed, precisely the kind of running that does the most for fitness and that builds a really good endurance base. However, if you do decide to do this, don't try to build up to a marathon in an unrealistically short time, and don't set time objectives until you've run your first one. Long-term goals should be just that—long-term. The length of time it will take you to work up to this sort of goal will vary with your condition, but trying to get there in a hurry will almost certainly defeat the purpose. Training mileages are discussed in detail later, and it is well not even to start thinking about a particular date or time period until you've built your regular distance up to twenty-five or thirty miles a week. Don't even think much about mileage until you find that you are jogging and running for a whole forty-five minutes each day. People who approach a marathon in this way are a lot more likely to enjoy the experience than those who are determined to crash their way into it.

Other goals may be equally worthwhile, whether they are short or long, ambitious or modest, provided you use them to give you encouragement on tough mornings, not to flog yourself forward at the limit of your endurance. Remember that enjoyment is the key. Save your willpower for occasional use, and concentrate on having a good time on most of your runs.

3/Shoes

Equipment plays a less important role in running than in any
other sport. The runner does not need a special place to run, a ref-
eree to judge his or her running, nor much in the way of specialized equipment. As a result, the runner is less affected by fashion
or the need to keep up with advances in technology and marketing.
You may buy the latest running suit, but you will go just as fast and
far in your old jeans. This is why the boom in running was ignored
until recently by the entrepreneurs of American sport—there
seemed little profit available.

The only real exception to the minimal importance equipment
has for the runner lies at the sole of the foot. Shoes are important,
and a lot of attention has to be paid to them. If you are going to
spend money on your running, spend it for shoes. The feet are at
the root of nearly all injuries and ailments suffered by runners.
Everything from painful knees to a sore back can usually be traced
to the manner in which the feet meet the ground. Ironically, a lot
of the problems are caused by shoes, yet they must often be solved
with shoes as well.

The foot is a beautifully designed instrument for running, but
it is abused so badly by civilized people that it often rebels and
usually requires a lot of protection to perform the functions for
which it was designed. We encase our feet in shoes that make
them sweat, soak, and become tender and that frequently deform
them or cause chronic injuries such as corns and bunions. We
allow our lower extremities to atrophy for years and then go out
and run long distances on hard pavement, instead of running
frequently for short distances on soft, irregular surfaces, as our ancestors did. The catalog of abuses is endless; the point is that most
of our foot problems are caused by the way we live. Such problems

are far less common among primitive peoples who go barefoot all day and who regularly walk distances that would make the average American drop to the ground in an exhausted stupor.

The usual solution to difficulties with the feet is a pair of well-chosen shoes. There may be good arguments for running barefoot instead, but that solution has not been well explored. It will be discussed briefly in another chapter and should probably be left by the beginner for later consideration. The novice has enough to worry about without adding that problem.

One thing we do know from the experiences of tens of thousands of runners is that shoes must be designed correctly. So many injuries have been caused by badly chosen footwear that you should pay attention to getting a good pair of running shoes quite early in your running career.

These days everyone knows what running shoes look like; they're those brightly colored nylon things with the snazzy contrasting stripes, and they are sold everywhere from specialty running shops to the corner drugstore. The problem is that most such "running shoes" aren't very good for running. They may be better than mountaineering boots, but they don't protect your feet from the pounding they take over months of training.

When you shop for a pair of shoes, start by thinking out what they're supposed to do. Running shoes should allow your feet to bend and flex through all the extreme motions they make while you are running with an absolute minimum of chafing, pressure, and effort beyond what is required to propel the body. The shoe should also cushion the foot as much as possible from the jarring impact of landing on pavement. Fine points in design and construction are important with running shoes because of the multiplying effect of the miles. Suppose you work up to a fairly modest routine of five miles a day. Each foot will then be hitting the ground about 120,000 times a month. At that rate, even a fairly small stress at each step can add up to more than your body can repair. A shoe that does not provide enough cushioning, pinches your toes, or requires your foot to push unnaturally to bend the sole can thus cause a lot of problems.

One happy by-product of the new popularity of running is the competition that has resulted in the manufacture of shoes for runners. Some real improvements have been made in the last few

During your running career, your feet will hit the pavement millions of times. Good shoes are important to minimize the stress on the body from this jarring.

years, and special shoes have been developed to meet unusual needs. This trend seems likely to continue, so more people will be able to run without suffering injuries because of badly fitting or poorly designed shoes.

It is important to remember that people's feet vary greatly and also that serious attention has been paid to running shoes only in recent years. A lot has still to be learned about the best ways to make them. Furthermore, since everyone's feet and body are different, answers that are developed are not definitive. The perfect shoe for someone else may not be a good one for you; in fact, the ideal shoe for 100,000 other runners may be a very bad one for you.

Fit

The single most important feature of the running shoe is the fit. No matter how good a shoe may be in all other respects, if it does not fit you well, wearing it will only be a torment. Finding a pair of shoes that fits well may be easy or difficult, depending on your own feet. For a long time, running shoes were nearly impossible to find in varying widths. Several manufacturers now make shoes in different widths, although you may have trouble finding the right one in a small shop. Other variations in foot structure may be harder to accommodate, and some people eventually have to buy custom inserts. Unless you have unusual foot problems, however, you should be able to find shoes that fit well by shopping around a little.

If you plan to wear socks while running (usually a good idea at the beginning), buy them before you go shopping for shoes so that you can try on the shoes with the socks you'll be wearing. Personally, I prefer lightweight soft wool or bulked Orlon socks. Many people like cotton because it absorbs perspiration well, but if your feet sweat a lot, you may find that cotton becomes abrasive once it gets wet. Pure nylon socks make the feet perspire a lot and should usually be avoided. Get socks that will stay up and that don't have lumps that will irritate the feet. Some runners prefer to wear the very low-cut socks that cover only the foot and have tassles on the heels to prevent their riding down.

Spend some time trying on shoes; don't try to rush out and buy a pair on your lunch hour. The best shops catering to runners will let you go out and jog around the parking lot or the block to try out the fit. At least try to run around the store a bit. The shoes should be snug at the heels so that your feet don't slip around in them. Movement inside the shoe will result in friction. That friction, innocuous as it may seem at first, will translate into a nasty set of blisters after you have been running awhile. The same caution applies to any little rough spots inside the shoes, particularly if you plan to run without socks.

You should have plenty of room around the toes; a tight fit there is likely to result both in blisters and bruised toenails. Your feet will swell during running with the increased supply of blood, and shoes that fit tightly in the store will become painful after a few miles. The area around the arch should feel comfortable and supportive. Unfortunately, you will find that most shoes have a very soft rubber arch cushion that is purely cosmetic, providing no real support when you are running. If your feet are flat or you have ever had arch problems, you should search out shoes that provide good support.

Modern running shoes should require no breaking-in to be comfortable and to conform with the feet. Most are made of nylon and will not stretch significantly, so tight spots will probably remain or rip out rather than gradually stretch. There are some good leather shoes on the market too. They are generally more durable than their nylon counterparts, and they have the virtue that they can be made water resistant for wet weather, but they do not breathe as well as nylon, are usually heavier, and will not dry rapidly. They may also develop folds or hard spots that will irritate the feet. If the advantages of leather are persuasive to you, treating the shoes regularly with leather preservatives will keep them pliable.

Don't rush into buying shoes if you can't find a good fit at the first store you try. It's better to run for a few extra days in your sneakers or old shoes than to run for months on end in a poorly chosen pair. Once you have found a pair of running shoes that meets your needs, you can keep buying the same kind and size, either locally or by mail, so the initial effort is well worth making.

Shoe Design

There are a number of features of shoe design that are always desirable, and many that are important to some runners but not to others. In general, shoe design is always something of a compromise among various desirable features, and an individual has to put a premium on the ones that best meet his or her needs. For example, light weight is very desirable in running shoes, as is good cushioning against the shock that results when the feet hit hard surfaces. Obviously, when more cushioning is added, weight is increased as well, assuming that the best available material is used. Thus, a balance has to be struck between two desirable features, and the optimum compromise will vary depending on the runner and the use to which the shoes are to be put.

Other choices in design may not be so much a question of balancing desirable qualities as of giving primary importance to the needs of some runners over others. A flared heel, for instance (discussed in detail later in this chapter), is quite helpful to some runners in stabilizing the foot as it strikes the ground; for others it is simply a nuisance that has to be cut off to prevent painful ankles.

For most runners the standard shoe is the training flat, a shoe substantial enough to be fairly durable and to give good protection, support, and cushioning to the foot. Training flats have soles suitable for running on any surface. The comments that follow refer to training shoes; spikes and racing flats, two other types of running shoes, will be considered separately in the chapter.

Materials. The *uppers* of most running shoes are now made of nylon reinforced at points of heavy wear with suede. The nylon is usually laminated with foam to form a sandwich. On the outside of the shoe is woven nylon cloth, then a thin layer of foam, and next to the foot a lightweight knit nylon.

The *heel counter*, which is the concealed stiffener that cups the back of the heel, is most commonly made of plastic. Plastic-impregnated fabric similar to that used on car upholstery is usually used to line the heel area. Trim and lacing hardware may be made of a number of materials.

As mentioned before, leather can be used to make good running shoes, which if treated properly with leather preservatives to prevent their drying out will provide long service. Leather is inherently more durable than nylon fabric, so leather has particular advantages for running in rough terrain. It is more difficult to make a leather shoe that will not irritate feet, though, and leather shoes tend to be heavier and more expensive than comparable nylon ones. For these reasons (and because a lot of people let their leather shoes dry out and develop hard spots), leather shoes have fallen out of favor.

Midsole. The midsole, a structurally important piece to which the uppers and the soles are attached, may be made of rubber, plastic, leather, or even cardboard. The uppers may be sewn to it, although they are usually glued. This attachment is made while the uppers are forced over a foot-shaped form called a last, giving the shoe its shape.

Insoles. Insoles can also be made of a variety of materials. The better ones are made of foam covered over with fabric. The best ones are nylon-covered neoprene foam, the same material that divers' wet suits are made of. (This type of insole is marketed separately by Spenco and is often called by that name.) Another good type is made of a plastic mesh that provides excellent ventilation under the feet.

Soles. Soles are made with several layers of synthetic rubber. The choice of the proper combination of sole materials is the most critical and sophisticated step in shoe design because these layers must provide traction, take most of the wear, and provide nearly all the cushioning the shoe gives the foot. The sole also has to be a stable platform for the runner and must flex easily where the foot does, to permit natural running. Basically, a tough synthetic rubber is used for the bottom layer to provide good wearing characteristics. This layer may also have special corrugations or other shapes molded in to provide mechanical cushioning by flexing, as well as giving a good grip. Ripple and waffle soles are examples. Additional layers between the midsole and this durable layer of rubber are made of much softer rubber or foam, which provides most of the cushioning. An extra wedge-shaped layer usually extends under the heel, which serves both as a heel lift and as an extra shock absorber for that part of the foot.

Cushioning. Perhaps the most important feature of training-shoe design is the cushioning that the shoe provides as the foot strikes the ground. Most runners spend a lot of their training miles on pavement and concrete, and the jarring impact of the foot striking such an unyielding surface, multiplied by hundreds of thousands of steps, can take a serious toll on joints and tendons. The cushioning in the sole of the training shoe is designed to alleviate the problems that can be caused by road shock. The amount of cushioning that is needed varies a good deal with the individual. Smooth runners who land lightly on their feet and aren't carrying a lot of body weight may be able to run comfortably with far less cushioning than heavier runners with a rougher running style. The amount of cushioning needed also tends to increase as the miles do. Shoes that are adequate when you are running four or five miles a day may not give you the protection you need to double that mileage.

To judge the cushioning that will be provided by a shoe, look first at the thickness of the sole. A heel that is one-half inch thick cannot cushion as well as one an inch thick; the greater the distance over which the foot is decelerated as it strikes, the more cushioning effect takes place. A really well-padded training shoe should have a heel that is nearly an inch thick and have a thickness under the ball of the foot of close to half an inch. Any shoe with cushioning less than three-eighths of an inch at the ball of the foot and three-quarters at the heel is too thin to be considered a training shoe. Lightweight runners who are easy on their legs may prefer cushioning at the lower end of the scale. Beginners are better off with more cushioning than they need, however, to prevent a beginner's mistakes from leading to chronic injuries.

The thickness of the sole is not an indication of good cushioning, only a prerequisite for it. To cushion against road shock, the sole must compress when the foot strikes the ground. Most shoes are designed so that nearly all the cushioning comes from a more yielding layer or layers between the midsole and the harder rubber that actually comes in contact with the ground. Typically, there is one cushioning layer the length of the shoe, or nearly the whole length, and an extra cushioning wedge from the heel to the front of the arch area. If you place your thumbs on the bottom of the sole near the edge at any point, you should be able to compress the cushioning layers to about half their normal thickness. If the layers are so hard you can barely dent them, as they are on most department-store "running shoes," there will be little cushioning effect.

Additional cushioning may be obtained from either a ripple sole or one with knobs of some sort molded into the running surface. Such soles have great value in providing good traction; the Nike waffle soles have long been a favorite of trail runners for this reason. The cushioning effect is likely to be short-lived, however, as the protrusions wear down at the points that hit the ground first. Be sure there is enough padding between the bottom surface and the midsole, rather than relying too heavily on the traction surface of the sole.

Both the heel and the ball of the foot should be well padded, at least for beginning runners. Joggers and most distance runners

The cushioning provided by the sole is critical. You should be able to dent it to about half its normal thickness by pressing with your thumb, using moderate force.

land primarily on the heel, drop the outside of the foot, then weight the inside, and finally take off from the ball with a drive from the toes. Making contact with the outside of the foot first (after coming down from the heel) and then rolling down the inside onto the ground is part of the foot's natural shock-absorbing mechanism, provided the motion is not too pronounced. Faster runners may land with the whole outside of the foot at the same time or directly on the ball of the foot, but novices will do this only if they are sprinting. If the heel strikes first, there is a lot of stress transmitted when it hits, and since the knee is also relatively straight, this shock is felt through the whole leg and hip. The padding at the heel is thus particularly important.

Some cushioning may be provided by parts of the shoe such as the insole, but the amount is bound to be quite limited, since even the best insoles are made from neoprene foam that is only an eighth of an inch thick. Most of the cushioning comes from the intermediate layers in the sole.

Flexibility. The flexibility of the sole is another feature important for the prevention of injury, and it is difficult to design a sole that is properly cushioned and also sufficiently flexible. Thickening the sole naturally tends to stiffen it. The place where the shoe has to be flexible is at the ball of the foot, where the foot itself naturally bends. A shoe that is flexible at the wrong spot may be worse than one that is uniformly stiff. If the shoe is excessively stiff, it will act somewhat like a platform, forcing the runner at each step to take off from the toes rather than from a platform made by the ball of the foot and the toes together. Coming up on the toes in an abnormal manner places a good deal of extra stress on the calf muscles and the Achilles tendon. The area of the Achilles tendon is a common injury point for runners, and a sole that is too stiff is a frequent contributor to serious problems.

Hold a running shoe in one hand and push the toe up to a ninety-degree bend with one or two fingers of the other hand. The shoe should bend where the ball of the foot comes, and the bending should not require too much effort. Compare a number of running shoes in this way and you will get some idea of the force needed and the relative flexibility of different shoes. Reject shoes that require a lot of force to bend the sole.

Heel lift. As a rule, you should be careful to get a running shoe that raises your heel at least as high above the ball of the foot as the shoes you normally wear. Runners tend to have tight tendons and muscles at the back of the leg because running naturally shortens the heel cords, calf muscles, and hamstrings. Wearing a running shoe with a lower heel than your street shoes may well contribute to injuries in these areas.

This recommendation needs to be qualified somewhat, as stretching exercises, which are strongly recommended later in this book, can extend these muscles and tendons, thus reducing the need for a good heel lift. However, most people already suffer from tightness in this area, and stretching takes time to work. A good wedge at the heel will help avoid injuries that take a long time to go away. Later on, if you develop good flexibility in this part of the leg, you can ignore this consideration in choosing shoes. For the great majority of runners, however, novices and veterans alike, proper lift is a very important requirement.

The actual height of the heel lift is the difference between the height of the heel and the height of the shoe at the ball of the foot, but it can usually be measured simply by checking the thickness of the foam wedge in the heel portion of the sole. Heel lifts can be purchased in many shoe-repair shops to go inside the shoes to provide more heel lift, but these may raise the heel of the foot too high inside the shoe, causing an improper fit.

Heel counters. If the heel of the foot drifts around inside the shoe, a number of foot problems can result. The heel should be held snugly in place with a stiff cup at the back of the shoe known as a heel counter. The heel counter should be stiff and resilient. It is normally made of plastic, covered with a smooth, tough, coated fabric inside the shoe and leather on the outside. Cheap shoes, which sometimes have cardboard counters instead of plastic, can be expected to deteriorate quickly. Lightweight leather alone will not hold up well. If the counter does not hold the heel snugly, you may later have to modify the shoe to correct the sloppy fit. Try to get shoes that have the proper heel width to start with.

Heel and sole flare. One of the problems that can result from thick soles is increasing instability of the foot, particularly the heel, as it is raised higher from the ground. This instability increases your chance of turning an ankle and also exacerbates problems caused by certain foot abnormalities. (Most people have some foot abnormalities, which frequently cause chronic problems for runners, a subject discussed in detail in chapter 9.) Heel and sole flares partly correct for this instability.

Some shoes have heels that widen out at the bottom to a really extreme degree, giving much the same impression as a dragster with tires eighteen inches wide. For some people, such shoes are a real blessing, stabilizing their landings and preventing the feet from bending over into positions that otherwise cause knee pain as daily mileage increases. The larger area may also improve sole wear, although many runners have to reinforce the points of high wear with glue (see page 64) to prevent the sole from rapidly wearing through at the spot where it hits the ground. Wide heels that are not glued may actually wear out faster than narrow ones, contrary to the manufacturer's claims.

Flaring may also permit the manufacturer to use a softer foam for cushioning, because the runner's weight is spread over a larger area, and the softer cushioning may retain resilience better. The wider sole does not provide more cushioning than a narrower sole of the same thickness, however, if both have the correct degree of hardness. It is the amount that the sole presses down vertically that provides the cushioning. The only sense in which the flare allows more cushioning is that it keeps a thick-soled shoe stable.

The flared sole is probably an advantage for the majority of runners, but for some it makes no difference, and for still others it causes problems rather than solving them. A number of runners experience pain in the ankles or in the legs just above the ankles when they wear shoes with flared heels, apparently because the wide sole at the point of contact forces the foot to pronate (roll inward) too quickly. If this is a problem, the protruding edges can be cut down with a razor blade or linoleum knife. Runners who find that the flared heel is a problem will naturally prefer shoes that don't have them in the first place.

Heel flare can correct for only a certain amount of imbalance, since the feet may also shift inside the shoes, especially if there are not good inside supports. Furthermore, on rough trails the flare may actually make it more difficult to get good footing, since the wide sole can serve to turn the foot to conform with an awkward angle on the surface as well as to flatten it when the trail is flat.

Support. In some ways the support that the shoe provides for the foot is a function of fit: the better the shoe fits the contours of the foot, the better the support it can give. Furthermore, since people's feet are not the same, shoes that may provide ideal support for one individual will be wrong for many others. For this reason it is commonly asserted that it is impractical to build arch supports into running shoes, because the supports needed by different people are so diverse. From a commercial point of view there is a lot of merit to this argument. There are limits to the number of variations that can be built into shoes and stocked in stores. It would be impossible for a store to stock each of a hundred models of running shoes in sizes ranging in length from women's size 4 to men's 14, widths from triple A to triple E, and arch-support heights from low to high. Still, it is quite possible that an innovative manufacturer could devise a way to get around this problem, considering the number of runners who find that they do need support, particularly in the area of the arch and inside forefoot.

Support around the heel by the heel counter has already been mentioned. Providing a slight cupping under the heel can also help to keep the heel in the proper position, a method used in the shoes designed by the great running coach Arthur Lydiard. As mentioned in the comments on heel and sole flare, the width of the sole also provides a firm platform for support, one that becomes more important with thicker soles.

The sole is also the first place to look in evaluating the support that a shoe will give to the arch. If the shank of the shoe is wide enough to extend out under the arch, then support inside the shoe can have some effect. If the sole is cut back under the arch to form a very narrow shank (known as a bridge), no supports that are put in the shoe can have any effect, because there is no foundation below to hold them up.

Nearly all running shoes have little sponge-rubber inserts under the arch that are quite soft and purely cosmetic. When you put on the shoes, these arch cushions may feel comfortably snug, but under the force of the descending body in running, they are compressed so easily that they provide negligible support. A lot of experienced runners simply rip them out after they buy new shoes and, if they need support, replace the sponge rubber with a more substantial substitute. (Some shoe modifications are discussed in chapter 9.)

Many people with so-called flatfeet or arch problems actually need support at the inside of the forefoot as much as or more than in the arch. The mechanics of the foot are one of the main subjects of chapter 9 and cannot be detailed here, but people with foot problems should remember that overall stability for the foot is important, and anyone with pain anywhere in the feet, legs, hips, or lower back should consider the feet as a possible source and corrective supports as a likely remedy. This is especially true of chronic knee pain.

A few brands of shoes give better than average support to the feet and are worth special consideration by anyone who suspects that his or her feet may be a problem. Etonic and Lydiard are particularly worthy of note.

Interior smoothness. Long-distance running with hot, sweaty feet guarantees a great deal of abrasion at any points on the feet that are rubbed even slightly with a single step. Even runners who wear socks find that spots suffering minor irritation at the beginning of a run can become sources of severe pain after five or ten miles on the roads. Many runners don't wear socks and therefore have a greater need for smooth inner-shoe surfaces. Pay a lot of attention to this matter when trying on shoes. Rough seams and fabric edges protruding into the shoe interior are typical problems. Terrycloth facing on insoles is less desirable than a slick nylon surface, although it will smooth out after twenty miles of running. Most tongues are slotted so that the laces can be threaded through to hold them high and straight, but if the tongue tends to work down easily or is sewn in crooked, so that it naturally gravitates to one side, it may irritate the top of the foot.

If you plan to wear socks for running, try your shoes on for fit with the socks, but give them a last check barefoot to detect any points of irritation that otherwise might show up only after several miles on the road. You can eventually develop calluses to protect your feet from such irritation, but good shoes shouldn't require you to.

Durability. Running shoes are expensive, so the longer they last, the happier you will be. Aside from the cost of replacing worn shoes, switching to new ones is something of a nuisance, and shopping for them requires time that could better be spent running. Unfortunately, durability can be only partly evaluated by simply looking at a shoe, and there is no source of data on the subject other than the reports of other runners. Good workmanship will obviously help keep a shoe from falling apart prematurely. Careful inspection of the seams and gluing should tell the runner how well the shoes were put together. Suede or leather uppers will outlast those of similar quality that are constructed of nylon. Nylon itself varies a good deal in quality, and the uppers of some shoes from reputable manufacturers deteriorate much more quickly than those from others.

The part of the shoe that is most vulnerable to wear is the sole. In general, soft sole materials will wear out more quickly than hard ones. Waffles, nipples, and other pointed patterns tend to wear quickly at first, because the stress is concentrated on the protrusions. When a small area wears down faster than the surrounding area, the angle at which the shoe lands can change and cause injuries. If, for example, you wear down the outside of your heel, you are likely to find that your legs begin to ache as soon as that side is three-sixteenths of an inch lower than the other. Partial or complete resoling may be needed fairly frequently if such wear occurs.

Proper application of glue (discussed later in this chapter) will retard sole wear. For this reason, I personally don't worry too much about sole wear in considering the durability of running shoes. Regular gluing usually makes my soles last as long as the uppers and layers of padding in the shoes. Runners who don't glue their soles, however, will want to consider durability of the soles a major economic factor when choosing shoes.

Two features that can't really be predicted except from use are the toughness of nylon uppers and the long-term resilience of the layers of padding in the sole. Nylon materials vary a great deal in durability and will wear out especially quickly if you run much in rough country where your shoes rub occasionally on rocks and are scratched by brush and thorns. For example, Nike Waffle Trainers are fine trail-running shoes, but nearly all the regular trail runners I know who use them have found that nylon wears through so quickly that they have to have leather sewn over the inside front panels as soon as they buy new shoes, to get proper wear from them.

Shock-absorbing layers in the sole will begin to fatigue and compress in time, particularly at the points of maximum impact. Such compression can gradually reduce the cushioning provided by the shoe and may also cause the shoe to cant one way or another, with the same potential for injuries as uneven sole wear. It is worth keeping an eye on shoes that are being glued or resoled to make sure that these layers are still in good condition.

Avoid cardboard layers in the insole or midsole, since they deteriorate badly, particularly if the shoes get wet often. Ask about the construction before you buy and look as carefully as you can. Assurances that there is no cardboard in the shoes can at least be used as a basis for demanding a refund if the shoes later fall apart and reveal such a layer. Peeling back the insole very slightly at a rear edge will often reveal the construction underneath. Terrycloth-backed insoles, besides being rougher than nylon-backed ones, often rot and crack before the rest of the shoe wears out. Nylon-covered neoprene insoles are usually still in good condition when the shoe falls apart.

Looking for a Bargain

Good running shoes are quite expensive. Competition in the last few years has improved quality and variety significantly, and there are signs of some competition in price since Brooks Company brought out some excellent training shoes at a much lower price than its competitors. Still, the price of shoes designed especially for runners will probably remain high because of the costs of advertising, development, and a natural yen for a good profit. What about the countless shoes aimed at the mass market that look almost the same as, and sell at a half or a third of the price of, the originals?

The novice to running may well be able to get by for a while with a pair of cheap shoes bought at the local discount store. Unfortunately, because of inexperience the beginner is also likely to run right into a chronic injury resulting from those same shoes, failing to recognize problems until they have become serious. I made exactly this mistake. Cheap shoes were perfectly adequate for me until my distance went over five miles a day, but I developed a severe inflammation of the Achilles tendon before recognizing that the shoes were no longer adequate. Some people might need good shoes from the very beginning, whereas others can seemingly run almost any mileage in any sort of shoe. Because of the problems that poor shoes can cause and the difficulty of judging them at first, the best advice seems to be to get good shoes when you start. In view of the problems that injuries can cause, the price is cheap.

It is sometimes possible to find real bargains in the mass shoe market, provided you are willing to spend some time searching them out. Such shoes are made in large quantities, generally in Hong Kong, Korea, and Taiwan, where labor costs are low. You cannot depend on brand names, because the various discount chains, department stores, and distributors who market these shoes will buy quantities from many different factories. Shoes that may seem superficially to be the same turn out on close inspection to be made from quite dissimilar materials. The same rack in the store may contain shoes that vary widely in quality.

Flared soles and heels have not yet filtered down to the mass market, nor has thick cushioning, so if you need stable or well-cushioned shoes, you might as well forget about the inexpensive varieties. Occasionally, some quite decent lightweight shoes with narrow heels and reasonable padding find their way onto the discount racks. If you want to try to find them, there are several things you should look for. Check the construction details carefully; no matter how low the price, the shoes will not be a bargain if they fall apart the first week. Compare the weight with that of regular running shoes; the cheapies are often much heavier despite minimal padding. Look at the insole; most inexpensive shoes have poor ones that may have to be supplemented with neoprene-nylon. Test the flexibility of the sole at the ball of the foot; if it does not bend up easily, it may cause tendon problems, though slashing lines across the sole with a razor or knife can partially alleviate this problem. Make sure the heel lift is as high as your street shoes unless you have flexible heel cords. Finally, check the softness of the padding layers in the sole, particularly the heel wedge. This is the major weak spot of almost all cheap shoes. The layers that are supposed to cushion your foot on impact are generally as hard as the roads you run on. If the shoes you've found satisfy all these tests and fit well too, you may indeed have uncovered a bargain.

Shoe Maintenance

Although running is one of the least expensive of sports, shoes are costly and they get a lot of wear, so it is worthwhile to make them last as long as possible. Soles can be replaced commercially, generally at rates in the range of half the price of a new pair of shoes. You can also buy some sole material and learn to do this job yourself if you are so inclined. It is not terribly difficult, since running soles are glued on, and little or no stitching is normally required. The best and simplest maintenance technique, however, seems to be regular application of adhesives to the points of wear. Proper use of glue should extend the life of a pair of soles to match the durability of the uppers, at much less expense and trouble than resoling. Some adhesives also make satisfactory major repairs on the uppers.

Several liquid adhesives—Shoe Goo, Sole Saver, and Sole Patch—are sold specifically for this purpose. They are somewhat expensive, but their main disadvantage is that after the adhesive has been applied, the shoes have to be left to cure for several hours, preferably for a whole day. I have also found that these adhesives did not adhere well to some of my soles. They do work very well for reinforcing spots on the uppers that are beginning to wear, and some runners use them regularly for sole maintenance.

In my experience the hot glue gun is the most satisfactory tool for minimizing sole wear. The glue gun is a small electrically heated appliance that melts cylindrical sticks of thermal adhesive of a type commonly used for constructing cardboard boxes. Both the glue guns and glue sticks are readily available in hardware stores and at many discount outlets. As of this writing a gun costs seven or eight dollars, and you should be able to get glue sticks in bulk for about a dime apiece. By fortunate coincidence, this type of glue adheres well to the sole material used in running shoes. It can be applied quickly, and the shoes can be used a few minutes later, as

Liquid adhesives sold specifically for the purpose can be used to keep the uppers of expensive running shoes in wearable condition. These well-worn running flats are a good example. Soles are best kept in good repair by using a glue gun.

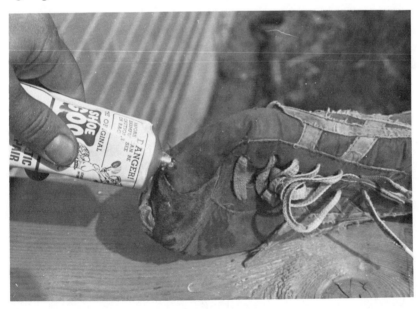

soon as the glue has cooled. Since using a glue gun will more than double the life of a pair of soles and the gun is cheaper than a resoling job, it will pay for itself with the first pair of shoes it is used on.

The principle of using any adhesive to prolong sole life is to begin applying it to areas of maximum wear from the time the shoes are new, using a thin layer of glue. This prevents major wear from ever taking place, so the soles never round off badly. When the patches of glue wear off, apply new ones. Depending on a host of variables, a glue patch may last anywhere from ten to a hundred miles of running.

The whole idea of using the glue gun is to keep the sole in its original configuration. It will wear down somewhat, of course, on parts of the sole not covered by patches and on occasions when the glue wears off in the middle of a run. You should never develop major low points in the sole, however, so the original shape of the bottom will stay the same for the life of the shoe. The overall tread wears down very slowly.

Don't apply the glue in thick blobs that raise one part of the sole above the rest, since high points can cause discomfort and injury as easily as low spots. As areas of secondary wear appear on the sole, thin layers of glue can be applied there too, always with the idea of keeping the sole configuration the same as it was when new. With waffle-type soles, one can either apply small amounts of glue to each tip quite frequently or simply fill in between the raised points at the areas of major wear. This really doesn't affect traction significantly, as most wear takes place over narrow areas where contact with the ground is first made.

If uppers begin to come apart long before they should, they can be patched with heavy nylon or with split leather (suede). It is best to patch early, before holes break through or become large. A heavy needle and thimble will normally do the job, though a shoemaker's awl or a Speedy Stitcher makes the job easier, particularly in hard-to-reach places near the toe. One can also take the shoes to a shoemaker, of course.

If the insoles of your shoes are made of cheap material, you may want to replace them with nylon-neoprene insoles either at the start or after the old ones start to come apart. The original insoles should usually be ripped out, unless the shoes are a little loose. Spenco insoles can be purchased, or you can save money by buying eighth-inch wet-suit material and cutting your own. Cut a pattern from cardboard first to avoid expensive mistakes. Many people simply insert insoles in the shoes, whereas others prefer to glue them with contact cement. Racers in particular may wish to avoid any possibility of the insoles slipping in the middle of a race. If you want to reuse the insoles, glue them in only a few spots.

Soles will not come loose from the uppers except perhaps a little at the toe if it catches on a rock. Minor gaps can be closed with contact cement or a glue gun. Larger ones are cause for returning the shoes, but if you do want to reglue them or to put new soles or heels on the shoes, the standard adhesive is Barge cement, obtainable at good hardware stores and from shoe-repair shops. As with all contact cements, the adhesive should be applied to both surfaces, previously roughened and cleaned. Allow the cement to dry before pressing the surfaces together. The surface of the cement starts to look dull instead of shiny when it has dried enough. Line things up correctly the first time, since the surfaces stick on contact. Make sure the whole sole has been well pressed down, perhaps by putting a hard object in the shoe and beating on the sole with a hammer.

Racing Shoes

Racing shoes can be classified into two broad categories: flats and spikes. Flats are rubber-soled shoes, as are training shoes, but racing models are lighter. They are used for road races, some cross-country courses, and running on some tracks with artificial surfaces. Spikes are the traditional track shoes, with six or seven sharp steel spikes under the forefoot to provide a good grip for racing on tracks and on dirt. Spikes for short distances, in which the racer is always up on the toes, have no heel lifts and little padding under the heel. Spikes made for milers and distance runners are a little heavier, with some heel lift and padding. There are also a few shoes with nylon nubbins rather than spikes for racing on artificial tracks.

The main requirement for racing shoes is that they be as light as possible yet still provide sufficient protection for the runner's feet to prevent injury. This is a difficult balance to strike, and each runner has to experiment in order to find out how light a shoe he or she can wear. There is no clear dividing line between racing and training flats, and the shoes that are sold by some manufacturers as racing flats are heavier than the training shoes of other makers.

Weight does make a real difference in the times of serious distance racers, but the beginner is well advised to ignore the problem and to race in his or her training shoes for a while. The weight of shoes is not likely to be a significant factor in performance until you have been racing seriously for a couple of years. The poor cushioning of a pair of light racing shoes may cause your legs to break down, however. By the time you have built your mileage up to that required for good racers, you will have a better idea of the support your feet need and will be able to experiment with lighter shoes.

4/ *Clothing, Weather, Traffic, and Man's Best Friends*

There are few important requirements for running clothing above the ankles, and tastes range from Saks Fifth Avenue tailoring to the Salvation Army reject bin. The main requirements are that your clothes meet the legal criteria for decency and that they not chafe or bind while you are running in them. Beyond these broad limits, the choice depends largely on the impression you want to make on the neighbors, if you care at all.

You should wear enough clothing to keep yourself reasonably warm without inducing any excess sweating. This can be a hard balance to strike, because you'll be a lot hotter after the first fifteen minutes than you were when you started, particularly if you choose to warm up by simply starting your run at a slow pace. If you run around the block or a track, you can simply shed a couple of layers after the first round or two. If you are running the roads, it is easiest to start off with a sweater or warm-up top that can be taken off and tied around the waist after you start to sweat.

Clothing naturally varies with the weather. When it's warm, you start off with the minimum that's feasible, taking modesty, the law, community standards, and protection from the sun into account. Women generally wear shorts with panties and a T-shirt or singlet with or without bra, depending on comfort and taste. Men usually wear shorts, an athletic supporter, and perhaps a T-shirt or singlet. Any shorts that don't irritate the insides of the thighs are fine. Nylon shorts that include an inner brief eliminate the need for underwear. They are comfortable, though expensive, and available in sizes to fit both sexes. Some women prefer leotard tops or stretch halters to keep their breasts from bouncing uncomfortably and to eliminate the need for a bra. When you start running, any shorts or cutoffs you have around the house will usually do. After you start to put in more miles, get something that doesn't rub.

In hot, sunny weather light-colored clothing reflects more heat away from the body, so it is preferable to dark garments. Cotton is best for absorbency, whereas nylon minimizes chafing. White nylon shorts and a lightweight white cotton shirt are a common compromise. Make sure you get enough ventilation around the abdomen. It is the most efficient place for your body to rid itself of excess heat.

Many people like to wear sweat-absorbing headbands, especially in hot weather. Others use wristlets covered with terry that can be used to wipe the brow, and still others carry a bandanna or rag tucked into the shorts for the same purpose. A light-colored hat with a brim to shade the eyes may be helpful on hot days, particularly if the top of your head is bald and subject to burning. Many runners use eyeshades when running in the sun. At any hot-weather marathon, you can find enough eccentric sorts of head-wear to satisfy all the clowns in a circus.

Depending on how vigorously you run, shorts and a T-shirt may be comfortable down to 50° F or a little cooler, once you have warmed up. When the weather is a bit too chilly for these you may be comfortable enough with the addition of a hat, generally a pull-over type of wool or bulked Orlon, or you may feel the need for some kind of longer clothing.

Warm-up suits of stretchy synthetic material are now quite familiar and are pleasant for running when the weather is a little too cool for short clothing. They are fashionable and rather expensive, so many runners use sweat suits or wear long underwear or pajama bottoms underneath regular running shorts.

Clothing for Foul Weather

Running in the rain is less of a problem than it might seem, because almost any clothing suitable for the temperature will keep you dry through your warm-up, and after that you will generate

Running clothing does not need to be elaborate. Shorts, a T-shirt, and appropriate underwear suffice in warm weather. The most important feature as the miles add up is that there be no rough seams or fasteners to irritate the skin.

enough heat to stay comfortable. Some kind of shell top, perhaps with a hood, is useful to shed the larger part of a downpour. Coated rainwear usually condenses so much moisture inside that it may be less comfortable than uncoated tight cloth. You will get wet in any case, and the object of a shell is simply to keep the rain from coming straight through. If the weather is warm, it is comfortable enough to run in light clothing despite the rain.

When the weather gets really cold, add a few more layers, preferably of a kind that can be taken off and tied around the waist when you want to do so. Several light layers are more comfortable and adjustable than one heavy one, and they are easier to dry. Gloves or mittens are important, since the hands, like the ears, are quite vulnerable whenever you get even a little chilly. If the weather is windy or may become so, be sure to wear an outer layer of clothing tight enough to turn the wind. In cold weather the dif-

ference between running with the wind at your back and its blowing into your face is enormous, and discovering it when you are
miles from home and damp with sweat can be a nasty experience.

Old sweaters, long underwear, or various other salvaged bits
of clothing can serve as insulating layers in really cold weather.
Wool and some of the bulked synthetics are preferable to cotton,
because they retain some insulating value when they get soaked
from sweat or falling snow. If the wind comes up or you get tired,
this can be important. For weather down to about 0° F (− 18° C), I
wear thermal underwear, regular running shorts, a sweater, a hat,
and gloves. I carry a light nylon windbreaker if I'm going far, in
case the wind comes up. For colder or windy weather I add wind
pants, an extra pullover, and a neck gaiter (described below).

A hat is crucial for temperature control in cold weather, and
face protection may also be quite important if the weather is very

As the weather gets cooler, the
runner simply adds layers to stay
warm. Clothing that doesn't bind or
chafe is important, and a series of
layers that can be stripped off is
preferable to a single heavy gar-
ment.

cold or there is blowing snow. Unlike other extremities, the head contains essential organs (though some people argue that the most important one is absent in runners). Because of this, the blood supply to the head is not reduced when the body becomes chilled, as it is to the arms and legs. Large quantities of heat can thus be lost through the head because of its ample blood supply. When you get chilly, a stocking cap is the most effective bit of insulation you can have, and it has the additional advantages of being compact and easy to take off and put back on as you get warmer or colder.

For face protection you may want a hat that incorporates a ski mask. I prefer the combination of a neck gaiter and a stocking cap, both because they permit more control and because they produce less fog on my glasses. A neck gaiter is simply a knit tube that goes around the neck and can be pulled up over the face for more protection. It can be purchased in some specialty shops or made from most stocking caps by removing the top ball and stitching.

Running in Cold Weather

In most parts of the country you'll have to get out and run in some fairly chilly weather if you want to stay in shape through the winter. Don't let this get you down. Cold-weather running is usually not unpleasant at all, not nearly so tough and hazardous as running in the heat. The body generates so much heat when you are running that staying warm is rarely a problem even in severe cold.

The biggest difficulties associated with cold-weather running are usually the peripheral ones: darkness, traffic, ice, and so on. Wintertime in the northern states means that the daylight hours are few. Many people can't run when it is light during the winter months because they are at work. Getting out at noon is more complicated in winter because of the extra time required to get in and out of wet clothing, the logistics of drying it, and similar difficulties. Running early in the morning or after work when it is dark and cold outside does require more fortitude than in the summer. Once you are on the road, winter running is usually quite pleasant, but getting out can be a trial. Keep it up anyway; it's a lot easier and more enjoyable than having to get back in shape in the spring.

You may need to change your running circuits for the winter. Pay particular attention to safety. Motorists are not alert for runners approaching them when the thermometer is registering subfreezing temperatures and snow is blowing around. People normally start driving before their defrosters really begin to work or their windshields are completely clear, and the most likely blind spot is on the side where an approaching runner would show up. Anticipate that you will not be seen, and be ready to make a dive into the ditch if necessary. Better yet, try to find routes that avoid getting close to cars during serious winter weather.

Aside from automobiles, ice is the biggest danger in the winter. Running in snow, slush, or water does not really present any serious problem, but ice is another matter. No matter how good your balance, a smooth patch of ice can cause you to take a nasty fall. Really icy conditions are one of the few things that should make you think twice about going out for a run. Traffic hazards are increased, and the danger of an incapacitating fall is serious. If you are running on ice, slow down, run flatfooted, and don't try to kick. Old lumpy ice on uncleared roads and sidewalks usually gives adequate traction, but it often can cause you to turn an ankle or twist a knee and should be negotiated with care.

Running in snow is far less of a problem, as long as it has not thawed and refrozen into a lumpy, corrugated surface. Just shorten your stride to match the effort required and keep your weight over your feet. The extra resistance and reduced traction will slow you down, of course, but running in snow can be delightful. Relax and enjoy yourself. Swinging through the powder on a cold winter night is absolutely exhilarating, and even splashing over the slush is not nearly as bad as you might think.

If temperatures are really cold or the weather is very bad, be cautious about getting too far from home. A runner in perspiration-soaked clothing has to keep moving to stay warm, and if the wind comes up with blowing snow when you are ten miles out on a country road, getting back can turn into an ordeal. It is often necessary to reduce mileage in the winter anyhow, because of the extra time and effort that may be involved in winter running. Make several short circuits instead of one long one if the weather is threatening.

No matter how cold the air is, you cannot freeze your lungs, even when you are breathing rapidly through your mouth. The air is adequately warmed by the time it reaches your lungs. You should be careful of colds, though, and avoid running in cold weather if you have any symptoms. The winter air tends to dry out the respiratory passages, besides cooling them. Take care to warm up after you finish a run, since it is easy to become chilled standing around in wet clothes. A hot shower when you get home is usually the best solution. In very cold weather (below − 10° F or − 29° C) hard breathing in the chilled air can lower body temperature rapidly, so it is important to be careful not to get too far from warm buildings until you know what you're doing. Wearing a face mask, neck gaiter, or something similar is usually necessary to avoid frostbite of the face, and the slight warming of the air before it is inhaled is of some help.

Running in Hot Weather

Hot-weather running needs to be approached with more care than cold, particularly when the humidity is high. Running in the heat places heavy demands on the circulatory system, as blood is shunted to the surface of the body to be cooled and heavy sweating removes large quantities of fluids from the body. The circulatory system also has to shunt liquids from one part of the body to another. Internal temperatures can reach high levels, and tremendous stress is placed on the whole organism. If the cooling system is overloaded, it can break down altogether, and only vigorous first-aid treatment will prevent death. Heat is particularly hazardous for those who have any cardiovascular disease. Overweight runners are also more vulnerable, because they have more difficulty dissipating heat.

All this is not to say that you shouldn't run if the temperature climbs above 70° F (21° C), but it is important to be aware of the extra stress that heat and high humidity impose on the body and to adjust your schedules and techniques accordingly. Unless you are in good shape already, try to avoid running in the heat of midday. Run in the cool of the morning or the evening. Make sure you have enough to drink, and take every opportunity to douse yourself with water. Reduce your training load. If you begin to feel dizzy, weak, clumsy, or strange, stop running, and walk to a shady place. Try to

Clothing for hot-weather running is simple enough, but heat is far more dangerous to the runner than cold. Even runners in good condition need to be wary of running long distances in the heat.

cool off in a sprinkler, a stream, or anything else available. On long runs, drinks that provide replacement for lost body salts are better than pure water. Salt alone should *never* be taken, and even water with only salt added is not a very good replacement. Potassium is as important as sodium, and potassium losses are increased by the ingestion of a saline solution. ERG, Body Punch, and diluted Gatorade are good replacement drinks, as is diluted tomato juice or slightly diluted orange juice with a pinch each of salt and baking soda. The Gatorade and juices are a little too strong for most runners unless mixed with water.

A discussion of heat acclimatization is included in chapter 11, but until you are in fairly good shape, it is probably not advisable to attempt to acclimatize to the heat. Try to keep the heat stress on your body to a minimum by running during the cooler hours, wearing the coolest possible clothing, getting enough to drink, and soaking yourself when you get hot. Slow down when the weather is hot, and don't go too far, especially without adequate liquid intake. Remember that heat stress is determined by both temperature and humidity. (When the humidity is high, perspiration evaporates more slowly and cannot cool you as well.) When both temperature and humidity climb to high levels, don't run until you are in good condition, and be cautious even then. A lot of world-class racers have nearly killed themselves in hot-weather races.

Traffic

If your house is surrounded by miles of smooth, soft-surfaced trails meandering through sweet-smelling pines, you can forget about the problems of running with traffic. If you are a beginner running only a few miles, you can also usually stick to the sidewalks, provided there are sidewalks where you live. Most runners covering very much distance in a week, however, end up spending a lot of time sharing roads with automobile traffic. It is important to keep reminding yourself that irrespective of intelligence, courtesy, or legal right-of-way, even the smallest car is a lot bigger, heavier, and harder than you are. There is no way you can win in a physical encounter. The road runner has to learn to be alert to traffic and to run defensively.

The safest attitude to take when you are running on roads is to convince yourself that every driver you encounter is either a homicidal maniac or is blind. Never assume that a driver sees you, understands what you are about to do, or will obey the law. Remember that you are betting your life when you run in front of a car.

When you are running on a road without sidewalks, it is generally safest to run against the traffic, on the left-hand side. If the traffic is light, you can run in the lane, moving over to the shoulder when you see a car approaching. With very light traffic and good visibility you can sometimes run the center line, avoiding the ankle strain caused at the edges by the crowning of the road, and staying in a position to move to either side to avoid occasional automobiles. In either of these cases, however, it is important to stay alert and not be lulled by the rhythm of your running, since a car moving at seventy miles per hour comes up very quickly. Even when you are running on the shoulder, be alert to jump out of the way of a car zooming along the edge of the pavement. Be particularly careful when rounding a blind curve.

Intersections are the most dangerous spots for the runner. Never assume that a driver will stop for a traffic light or a stop sign. Typically, when a runner is jogging along the left side of the road, a driver coming out of a side road from the left will look the other way at oncoming traffic to make a right turn and will never check for pedestrians on his right. Thus, the driver may run you down without ever glancing at you if you proceed in front of the car, whether it is moving or stopped. Make eye contact with the driver before you run in front of the car. With a car stopped at an intersection, knocking on the hood is a good way of getting the motorist's attention.

It is also important to remember that many drivers literally will not see a runner. They are tuned in to cars and other large objects and their minds simply don't register the presence of a runner. Furthermore, even if you are seen, the typical driver will consider you to be a stationary object, not moving fast enough to take account of your speed. Thus, a driver making a right or left turn from a main highway will often hit a runner from behind because the motorist won't allow for the runner's motion. The accident will be the driver's fault, but that will not do the runner much good. Look behind as well as ahead before you cross a side street, and always assume the worst.

If you run on the roads at night, early in the morning, or during bad weather, you should pay some attention to your visibility as an aspect of running defensively. Running in dark clothes in the middle of the night is likely to be suicidal. Even a motorist who is watching carefully will not spot you until practically on top of you. The average driver, who is not alert for runners in the daytime, much less in the middle of the night, will run you down without even noticing. Dark clothing is good in the snow, but most of the rest of the time, white or light yellow clothing is the minimum requirement for visibility. Runners who habitually get out on dark roads should buy or make some items of clothing with reflective material that shows up in the slightest glimmer from a car's headlights. It is a good idea to have reflective strips on several parts of the body, easily visible from all angles. Strips on the arms, legs, or feet will move when you are running and may help attract extra attention.

Gimmick lovers may have the ultimate answer to the problem of attracting the attention of motorists: a battery-powered strobe light can be carried in one hand and turned on when necessary. Such a light emits a series of bright flashes, each of short duration, so that excessive power is not used. Most runners are likely to reject such technological gadgets, but the extra safety margin they provide those who run the roads at night is considerable. (An inexpensive, lightweight strobe that will clip to a belt or waistband is made by Ampec, Inc., Box 15461, Phoenix, AZ. 85060.)

Dogs

Dogs can be a major hazard to runners. A runner going by on the sidewalk or road is often considered by a dog to be challenging his territory. As a running animal, you may also arouse an instinctive hunting reaction. Finally, to add insult to injury, a runner attempting to defend himself or herself from an attacking dog often arouses the ire of the animal's owner. The fact that poor Fido has just chewed a hunk out of your leg, or tried to, does not seem to the owner sufficient cause for you to hit him on the nose or spray repellent on him. I know at least one runner who was assaulted by the owner of a dog he had hit while he was being attacked.

Most dogs pose no threat at all and are either friendly or merely noisy. Bites or injuries sustained while trying to avoid the exceptions can be serious, however. Furthermore, a bite that breaks the skin can result in the necessity of a painful and dangerous series of rabies inoculations unless the animal can be identified and captured. The problem is compounded because in many areas both the legal authorities and the dog owners have refused to provide any relief against the danger.

Pay some attention to dogs along your route. The really vicious ones often don't bark at all and will sneak up on you from behind. Most of the time, a dog won't attack if you are facing it, particularly if you don't show fear. Most dogs are rather cowardly and are perfectly happy to put on a good show of barking while letting you go your way, provided you don't turn your back. Those that are a bit more aggressive will still usually be discouraged if you make a show of picking up a rock or pretending to.

When you are running along routes that are unfamiliar or that you know have vicious animals along the way, carrying some means of self-defense may be advisable. An automobile battery terminal clamp or a large lead fishing sinker on the end of a piece of cord can be swung around in a circle and makes an effective weapon. (Cover the weight with tape so that lead doesn't rub off on your hands.) Two lengths of dowel connected with a short piece of cord can also be carried easily and swung at the snout of an attacking dog.

When dogs are a major problem, particularly if you are bothered every day by the same animal, a pressurized canister of Mace or Halt (sources discussed on page 114) is probably the best solution. Once a dog has been sprayed with one of these substances, he will usually keep clear of runners for a few months.

All these comments apply only to naturally aggressive animals. If you have a problem with a hostile owner or a trained attack dog and survive the first experience, don't return to the spot until something has been done. Call the police and demand some action, then make sure you get it. If you should be bitten, call the authorities immediately. If the dog was rabid, there is a danger of your contracting rabies, which is fatal, and the normal medical procedure is to give the victim of a bite a series of quite unpleasant injections, unless the animal can be found and confined to determine whether it has the disease. It is therefore important to you that the dog be caught so that you won't have to have the shots. If you get a bite from any animal that cannot be caught or located, see a doctor.

5/
Training Principles for Beginners

Understanding the basic changes that occur in the body as it adapts to the stress of running is useful because it can help you modify your running habits to achieve the results you want. Perhaps more important, it adds another dimension to the experience of running. By adding to your comprehension of what is going on in your body, it enhances your awareness of the relationships between the physical, mental, and emotional selves. This feeling of integration of mind and body can be one of the great rewards of running.

Training is a term that has bad connotations for some people because of its association with painful episodes under authoritarian coaches or army drill sergeants. Some forms of training for runners may be boring, but there is usually no need for them to be, particularly for adults running because they want to. Training your body means directing its growth, in terms of both skill and physical development. Intelligent training will speed progress toward the goals you have in mind at a given time. Such training will certainly involve work, but it does not have to be unpleasant, particularly as your level of fitness improves. Enjoyable runs through the woods can train your body in the direction you choose just as well as endless repetitions of laps on a track. One of your most important training goals should be to enjoy each day's session as much as possible. By making your training a pleasure, you'll keep it up.

Aerobic and Anaerobic Exercise

The distinction between aerobic and anaerobic states is a fundamental one. Aerobic activity takes place in the presence of a supply of oxygen. Anaerobic processes take over when not enough oxygen is available. The muscles have to burn fuel in order to do any kind of work: walking, running, lifting weights, or doing dishes. The energy required to do the work is extracted in the muscles themselves, from the food you eat after the digestive tract has converted it to usable form and the blood has carried it to the muscles. The energy is stored in the chemical bonds of this food, and a complicated series of chemical reactions allows the body to extract this energy at a controlled rate. In the process the food is oxidized the way fuel is burned in a fire, except that the body combines the oxygen and fuel in steps, so that energy is released at the rate it is needed. Oxygen is a vital ingredient of this basic metabolism of food, just as it is required for a fire to burn.

Since the rate at which oxygen can be supplied to the muscles is limited and requires some time to speed up when demands are increased, the muscles are also able to derive energy from food for a brief time without using oxygen. Without having to breathe hard in advance, you can summon a sudden burst of energy that your ancestors used to escape from danger or to attack their prey. After this quick burst, however, the hard breathing that was postponed has to be done. This capacity for doing work without oxygen is strictly limited; for sustained effort, oxygen has to be supplied as rapidly as it is used.

The reactions that take place when the muscles are working aerobically are completely different from those occurring in an anaerobic state. Besides building up an oxygen debt, which has to be repaid, anaerobic exercise produces waste products (particularly lactic acid) that cause rapid fatigue and inability to work if they build up in any quantity. Thus, doing very much work anaerobically quickly exceeds the body's capacity to recover without a long rest period. The chemical reactions involved in exercising anaerobically are also far less efficient than aerobic ones. Much more glycogen (the fuel used by the muscles) is required to perform an equivalent amount of work.

A fast sprint at maximum speed is a typical example of anaerobic exercise. If you really go all out, you will collapse into a panting heap in a few hundred yards at the most. The hundred-yard dash is a typical athletic event that is almost wholly anaerobic. The sprinter could run almost as fast holding his or her breath through the entire hundred yards, building up an oxygen debt that has to be repaid in the gasping period after the race is over. On the other hand, long-distance runs are almost wholly aerobic, because it is impossible to go very far except by supplying oxygen to the muscles as you go.

Training can be classified as aerobic or anaerobic, depending on the sort of exercise that you do. Short bursts of anaerobic work, as in hitting a golf ball and then watching its trajectory, or pushing a heavy weight up once or twice, may increase strength in the muscles used, but they have virtually no effect on the capacity of the body to make prolonged efforts. They don't present the right kind of stress, as we shall see. Even sprints or the intermittent efforts required in most team sports have little effect on endurance. They are mostly anaerobic, and oxygen is repaid during the following rest period.

Stress and Adaptation

Your body is a remarkably adaptive organism. Over a period of time, a middle-aged person who is overweight and completely out of condition can progress from a state in which it is impossible to sustain a brisk walk for more than a block to one in which he or she can run a marathon at a good pace. Thousands of people have demonstrated this.

The basic ingredient of physical training is stress. If you stress your body by doing something that is difficult but not so difficult as to cause injury, your body will adapt to the stress. It will become stronger in whatever way is required to cope with the stress you apply. A regular increase in the stress experienced will gradually force your body to become stronger and stronger, provided you stay within its adaptive limits. If you increase the stress too quickly, you'll get hurt.

An obvious example of this principle is the idea of weight training, in which the weight or the number of repetitions is slowly

The body is a remarkably adaptive organism; it responds to stress by becoming stronger. Running is thus both an aesthetic experience and a personal experiment in training the body toward its physical limitations.

increased as the muscles used get stronger and stronger. The key to all training is knowing what kind of stress to put on the body to achieve the desired results and knowing how fast to increase the load.

Applying the right kind of stress is vital. Push-ups are a superb exercise if you want to strengthen your arms and shoulders, but they don't improve your cardiopulmonary fitness unless you can do a few hundred in a row. The body adapts only to the stresses applied. To develop a stronger heart, better circulation, and a more efficient breathing apparatus, you must do work that challenges your capacities in those areas. You have to do something that makes your heart beat faster for a long period and that forces you to breathe hard.

The reason that running is such a good form of exercise for overall fitness is that it places stress on just those systems: the heart, blood vessels, lungs, and a number of the large muscles. Distance running in particular stresses the body in those areas. Running will not enable you to do more push-ups, but it will strengthen your heart and lungs so that any work you do will be easier on these vital systems.

The rate of adaptation is a second critical factor in any training program. For the world-class athlete, the optimum training program is one that will force the body to adapt at its maximum capacity and to reach the highest level of fitness on the days of the most important competition; it is the program that falls just short of causing serious injury. A slight miscalculation pushes the athlete's body over the line and something breaks down. Competitors of this caliber are always pushing the limits, finding out how much stress they can force their bodies to adapt to. Most of them sustain a lot of injuries in the process.

For the beginner, particularly one beyond the age of twenty-five or so, this kind of training makes no sense. One of the key features of any training program should be to avoid injuries. If you hurt yourself, your goals will be set back for long periods. Overstress in early stages of a training program can involve serious risks. Besides, who needs the pain? The old macho athletic myths that training does no good unless it hurts are nonsense. Willpower and hard work are needed, but real pain is a sign that your body is being broken down rather than built up. Be conservative in the strains you impose on your adaptive abilities, particularly at the early stages. You have plenty of time to reach your goals, and there is no sense in pushing too fast. Most of us are impatient when we decide to do something. We want instant results in everything. When we decide to do something about our physical condition, we expect to be able to make up for decades of neglect in a few hours, days, or months. This approach will not work. The body will only adapt slowly to regularly applied stress. You can't cheat. If you don't keep at it, preferably every day, your body won't bother to respond. If you try to increase the load too quickly, it will respond by breaking down.

Strength and Endurance

Strength is an imprecise term, but we usually use it to denote the amount of force a person is capable of exerting—to lift a weight, for example. It is typical of the body's mechanisms for adapting to stress that training for maximum strength has almost no carry-over into the area of endurance, and vice versa, just as building the strength of the legs has no effect on the arms. Lifting heavy weights, shot-putting, sprinting a hundred yards, or doing isometric exercises will increase the strength of the muscle groups involved, but none of these activities will build endurance either in those muscles or in the respiratory and circulatory systems.

The type of exercise that forces the body to function more efficiently in getting oxygen to the muscles and processing it is sustained movement of a number of the large muscles of the body at a high enough level of activity to make the heart and lungs work hard. Bicycling, swimming, cross-country skiing, running, walking, rowing, or paddling are examples of such activities *if they are carried on vigorously enough.* An experienced swimmer moving along easily with a breast- or sidestroke will not produce any conditioning effect for the cardiopulmonary system, nor will a casual walker or cyclist.

Obviously, both strength and endurance are necessary for any reasonable definition of fitness, the mixture depending on individual needs and desires. But it is endurance training that builds cardiopulmonary fitness and has the most important effects on overall health. This is the sort of fitness that distance running builds, although it makes essentially no contribution to the ability of the muscle for weight lifting or arm wrestling. Specific kinds of training are necessary to build muscle strength and endurance, and they are quite different.

Body Changes during Training

Regular endurance training has profound effects on the way the body functions and on its makeup. The volume of blood pumped by the heart during each stroke is increased, and as a result the heart pumps more slowly to sustain a given level of circulation. Blood circulation within the heart itself improves. The amount of air that can be taken in with each breath increases, as does the capacity for breathing large quantities of air over a long period of time. The circulation in the working muscles improves, and the ability of the muscles to utilize oxygen becomes greater. The muscles themselves become more efficient, and more of the contracting fibers that drive the body forward fire in unison. As the body gains the ability to do more work, lower levels of effort are performed more efficiently, requiring not only a smaller percentage of the body's capacity but also a smaller absolute expenditure of energy.

A person who is running regularly also tends to lose weight if, like most Americans, he or she is carrying much extra fat. This is true primarily because of the extra energy used for daily running. (The complicated relationships between weight, fat, and running are discussed later in this chapter.)

Oxygen Uptake

The quantitative measure that best reflects the combined work of all parts of the cardiopulmonary system is oxygen uptake, the amount of oxygen actually consumed by the body in a given time. The maximum oxygen uptake that a person can achieve correlates with the amount of work he or she can accomplish, and the degree to which this maximum uptake can be sustained for long periods of time is a good index of endurance fitness.

Measuring oxygen uptake requires laboratory instruments and procedures, and even though you will probably never have your uptake measured directly, there is a lot to be learned from studies that have been made of it. The amount of oxygen you remove from the air is measured when you are exercising at the highest level you can. The difference in results between trained and untrained people is remarkable. The typical adult will have a maximum oxygen uptake of twenty-five to forty milliliters per minute for each kilogram of body weight, whereas a highly trained endurance athlete will be able to process seventy to eighty milliliters per minute per kilogram. Any healthy adult who takes up an endurance training program can greatly increase his or her maximum uptake. For those interested in racing, oxygen-uptake capacity correlates well with distance-racing success. By increasing your capacity you will effectively increase your speed.

Virtually all training for beginning runners should be aimed at increasing oxygen uptake. This is true whether you are interested in running primarily for fitness, for sheer enjoyment, or as background training for racing. The cardiopulmonary fitness reflected in a high maximum oxygen uptake is almost a definition of fitness in the broad sense that applies to nearly all activities.

From the standpoint of enjoyment, it is adequate oxygen uptake that lets you enjoy the physical pleasures of running, rather than struggling for breath and tiring after only short jogs. Most seasoned runners have found that the real pleasures of running are most often experienced during long runs, after one has gotten up to at least five miles in a session. But this enjoyment is not felt until you have built up enough aerobic fitness to make such long runs with relative ease.

Finally, if you want to compete, regardless of whether you want to run short races or long ones, speed is best built up from a strong foundation of cardiopulmonary fitness resulting from long miles of training.

Pulse Rates

One of the best indexes of oxygen uptake, fitness, and improvement in condition is your pulse rate. One of the well-known attributes of endurance athletes is a very low resting pulse, sometimes as low as twenty-five or thirty beats a minute, compared with average adult rates in the seventies. The reason that the pulse rate usually declines as conditioning improves is that the volume of blood pumped by the heart with each stroke increases so that the number of beats required to maintain normal circulation is reduced. For example, if twice as much blood is pushed out with each stroke, the heart needs to beat only half as fast. Other factors, such as an increase in red blood cells (which transport oxygen from the lungs to the tissues), play a lesser role.

This increase in the stroke volume of the heart, which is commonly accompanied by an improved blood supply within the heart itself and increased strength in its walls, is one of the factors con-

tributing to greater oxygen-uptake capacity. Unlike maximum uptake, however, the resting pulse rate does not have to be determined with expensive laboratory equipment. It can be taken
accurately using any watch or clock with a sweep second hand. It
would be misleading to compare your pulse with someone else's to
gauge your relative fitness, but checking your own resting pulse
occasionally can be a good indication of improvement. A sudden
increase in resting rates also provides a good warning sign of illness
or overtraining; it can be an instruction from your body to take a
rest.

For a comparable resting pulse, it is best to check the rate
when you wake up, before getting out of bed, when the pulse is
normally lowest. Rates during the day will vary somewhat depending on recent activity, eating, coffee drinking, and the like. It's
easy to learn to take your pulse, and it can be particularly worthwhile if you are in poor shape, since pulse rates can be used to regulate your level of exercise. The two most convenient spots for taking your pulse are the wrist and the neck. Experiment with both to
find out which is easier for you to use. In either case, use the first
two fingers of one hand; the thumb is not good for feeling a pulse
because the pulse in the thumb itself is often strong enough to be
confused with the beats you are trying to count. To take the pulse
at the wrist, place the tips of your fingers in the groove on the
thumb side of the raised central tendons on the inside of the wrist,
about an inch from the hand. Feel around a little until you find a
clear, steady beat. To take the pulse at the neck, you need to press
a little deeper to find the carotid artery, which supplies the brain.
Place the tips of your fingers lightly on the Adam's apple and slide
them straight over to one side past the hard windpipe and into the
first soft, deep area. Press lightly and feel around until you find the
pulse. Never press on both carotids at once, lest you cut off circulation to the brain. Once you have the rhythm of either pulse, count
the beats for a full minute to get the most accurate figure.

Pulse rates taken at various times can be most revealing. An
especially accurate indication of your level of conditioning is the ra-
pidity with which your pulse drops to a normal rate after hard exercise at a particular level. This drop indicates that the oxygen debt
acquired during the effort has been paid back. Similarly, a high
rate continuing long after the exercise is over is a sign that it was

quite taxing. Exact figures depend on your own resting and maximum rates, on the duration of exercise, and similar variables. For the average person, however, the pulse should have fallen below a hundred beats per minute within ten minutes after a daily workout. The pulse will not return to normal for some time after this, but if it stays above a hundred for more than ten or fifteen minutes, either the workout was too hard or the runner is suffering from some illness. Overtraining over a longer period may also be reflected in a slow recovery rate.

By taking your pulse during exercise, you can find out how much stress you are putting on your system. It is usually not very practical to try to take a pulse on the run, but a fairly accurate figure can be obtained by getting the fingers in position, stopping, counting the pulse for the first ten seconds, and multiplying by six. The reason for the short duration is that the pulse slows rapidly after you stop, particularly if you are in good shape, so the multiplied short count is more accurate than a longer one. This pulse can be used to gauge the strenuousness of the exercise and thus both its conditioning effect and the hazard it might pose to a person with heart disease.

The maximum rate at which the heart beats varies somewhat from person to person, but the typical high for a twenty-year-old would be 200 beats per minute. In older people the maximum declines a little less than 1 beat for each year. A reasonable estimate of your maximum heart rate can thus be obtained by subtracting your age over twenty from 200. A thirty-five-year-old might estimate the maximum at 185 and a sixty-five-year-old at 155. These figures are approximate, but they work fairly well for the purposes discussed below.

A person's maximum heart rate does not increase with training. Additional capacity for processing oxygen is achieved through increasing stroke volume, larger numbers of capillaries in the muscles, greater lung capacity, and similar changes. The greatest efficiency in processing oxygen is likely to be achieved at a heart rate slightly below maximum, since the stroke volume begins to decline at rapid rates. In fact, highly trained endurance athletes seem to have slightly lower maximums than the average for their ages, although this may result from the difficulty in pushing them to true maximum levels.

One reason for being interested in maximum heart rate is that it can be used to estimate the effect that a certain duration of training will have in stimulating the body to become more fit. The more the body is stressed, the greater the training effect. At low levels of stress, on the other hand, there is virtually no training effect. In order to gain in cardiopulmonary fitness, a person needs to exercise so that the pulse rate is over a certain threshold.* The threshold can be expressed in this formula:

$$P_t = P_r + 0.6\,(P_m - P_r)$$

where P_t is the threshold pulse, P_r the resting pulse, and P_m the maximum pulse, determined either by testing or by using the rough method mentioned above. Thus, a person 35 years old who finds that his or her resting pulse is 72 could calculate the threshold pulse for training by first estimating the maximum pulse at $200 - 15 = 185$, 15 being the years over 20. The formula then yields

$$
\begin{aligned}
P_t &= 72 + 0.6\,(185 - 72) \\
&= 72 + 0.6\,(113) \\
&= 70 + 68 \\
&= 138
\end{aligned}
$$

A more highly conditioned person the same age with a resting pulse of 45 would have a threshold of 129.

A greater conditioning effect is achieved when the exercise pulse rate is closer to the maximum. Levels of exercise that normally do not raise the pulse above the threshold have a conditioning effect only if they are continued for extended periods. Frequently, by the time such extended exercise has taken place, the pulse may in fact have risen above the threshold because of fatigue. During exercise periods lasting between ten minutes and a couple of hours, however, the heart rate should be above the threshold rate for much of the time if any conditioning is to occur.

For beginners, particularly those who are not very fit or who are over the age of thirty-five, the pulse rate should not go very much above the threshold level during the first few weeks or

* The formula and discussion here are derived from H. A. De Vries, *Physiology of Exercise for Physical Education and Athletics* (Dubuque, Iowa: Wm. C. Brown, 1966). See also David L. Costill, *What Research Tells the Coach About Distance Running* (Washington, D.C.: American Alliance for Health, Physical Education, and Recreation, 1968).

months of training, and it should reach the threshold only part of the time. After you've walked or jogged fast enough to be breathing deeply, stop for a few seconds and take your pulse. If it's above the threshold level, walk moderately for a while to allow your body to recover. You'll find after a few weeks that more and more effort will be required to get the pulse up to the same level.

After a longer period the numerical value of the threshold will drop as your resting pulse is reduced. For trained people, the ideal training pace is often much faster than the walking and jogging routine mentioned above, but the novice should work up slowly, particularly if he or she is older or very much out of condition. Even for those in good shape, extending distance rather than increasing speed is a good basic rule, as long as you are moving fast enough to bring your pulse above the threshold level.

If you are interested in following your own progress, you can record your pulse rates after running, walking, or jogging over a set course at a set pace. After a period of weeks or months, you will find that the course will not only feel much easier but your pulse rate will be lower to accomplish the same task. Don't get fixed on numbers so much that you try this every day or week, however. An obsession with daily variations is pointless and is likely to be discouraging; you'll be observing the effects of last night's party or this morning's breakfast rather than last month's training. The only point of frequent pulse taking is to monitor the level of exercise for those worried about overstressing themselves.

Fat

Americans eat a lot more than is good for them. Their meals are often nutritionally unimpressive but frequent. Most people put on a fair amount of weight after they have physically matured, and with rare exceptions it is all fat. In many cases, this weight is added to padding that was already acquired in childhood and adolescence. The reasons for this are fairly simple. The average mature person becomes less and less active as he or she gets older but does not reduce food intake an equivalent amount. If you take in more calories than you use up, the extra energy is stored as fat, mostly in folds under the skin. This was a useful survival technique for earlier generations, who frequently had to use that stored fat as fuel to tide them over the lean months, but it is not so good for modern man.

There is nothing wrong with fat per se. It is an excellent concentrated food for many purposes. Teaching the muscles to burn fat seems to be one of the mechanisms involved in training to run long distances. The heart, which is the archetypal endurance muscle, burns fat in preference to carbohydrates. Fats that are stored for ready use and then burned in this way have to be distinguished from the kind that most of us carry around, however. All that excess tissue that we build up from eating too much and doing too little is an extra burden on the organs of the body. It has to be supplied with oxygen, nutrients, and other necessities. It has to be lifted when we move, encouraging many to move even less. There is little doubt that the combination of excessive weight and inadequate exercise is one of the main reasons—if not *the* reason—for the incredible increase in cardiovascular diseases that plagues us. Starting from an early age, we begin to build up fatty deposits inside our arteries, including those that supply the brain and the heart. Eventually there is no longer space for an adequate blood supply to pass through. Although the mechanism of accumulation of these plaques is not completely understood, there is little doubt that overeating and inactivity are major contributing factors.

Running can be a big help in controlling weight and appetite, provided you understand the mechanisms involved and don't expect miracles. A running program can also be a big help in conjunction with a diet to help those who want to lose a lot of weight more quickly and in the right places. Running will *not* miraculously melt the pounds away, particularly for the beginner who can cover only a few miles a day. It can best be used to burn large numbers of Calories by those who are well conditioned and least need to do so. (A Calorie, spelled with a capital C, is the normal unit used to measure the energy available in foods. It is the amount of energy required to heat a kilogram of water 1° Celsius and is equal to a thousand calories, the conventional unit used by physical scientists.) This does not mean that running is not useful for weight reduction, however. On the contrary, it is far more effective in the long run than all the quick-loss fad diets, thyroid injections, and amphetamines in the world.

Many people argue that exercise is ineffective in weight control, because only a small number of Calories are used up. For example, a person of average weight will use up roughly 100 Calories in running a mile, over a fairly wide range of speeds. Shedding a pound of fat requires that you burn about 3,500 Calories (the same amount you ate to put it on). Thus, you have to run 35 miles to take off a pound, a discouraging fact indeed for those searching for quick weight loss.

The dilemma of most people who have trouble controlling their weight, though, is that they cannot get their energy output to match their caloric intake on a long-term basis. They diet for a while, lose a few pounds, and then put them right back on, which is probably unhealthier than leaving the extra weight there in the first place. The caloric requirements of exercise look very different when viewed from the perspective of the regular runner. A person running twenty-five miles a week, which is a fairly modest distance after a little training, can lose thirty-seven pounds in a year while eating the same amount as before. More important, by maintaining the running habit, he or she can avoid immediately gaining it back.

The most important influence of running on weight is that of increasing energy output to match more closely caloric intake, but it is helpful in other ways as well. Prolonged exercise acts as an appetite depressant. Although a walk around the block is likely to stimulate your appetite, an hour's run will generally make you less hungry. For those who are seriously trying to control their weight, a major advantage can be gained by timing the daily workout to come around the time of a meal or a snack so that they will be inclined to skip it or reduce the amount eaten.

In conjunction with a diet, running is also helpful not only in burning extra calories but in channeling weight loss. The typical person on a crash diet loses muscle tissue as well as fat. When he or she starts eating again, most of the weight gained is fat. This is one reason why alternate heavy dieting and heavy eating is dangerous. On the other hand, a person who is exercising while dieting tends to burn off fat rather than muscle tissue. This is why so many people on crash diets feel poorly before and after diets, whereas dieting runners generally do not feel weaker at all. Furthermore, since fat occupies far more space per unit weight than muscle, it is possible to become much trimmer on a conditioning program even without weight loss.

Good distance runners have remarkably low percentages of body fat.
The fat that is stored beneath the
skin when we eat more food than
we burn up is a drain on the body.
Running can be an important aid
in getting rid of fat.

Finally, running can play an important psychological role in
weight control. You cannot help being aware of the influence of
weight on performance when you are running. It slows you down!
The knowledge that you will run better and with more pleasure if
you trim down a little can be a powerful motivation. Yet the runner
does not usually develop the kind of unhealthy obsession with
weight that is a problem for many overweight people. The knowledge that you are getting fitter is pleasant in itself, which makes it
easier to motivate yourself to lose weight and keep it off without
feeling the need to become slim *now*.

It is important, however, not to try to turn your running program into another form of crash diet. The beginner who is out of
condition and who goes on a severe diet is not likely to be able to
go out and start a difficult regimen of running at the same time. If
you aren't very much overweight, probably the best tactic is to
start running first, while not eating any more than you normally

do. This in itself will make slow but definite inroads against your belt line. Furthermore, as you get in better shape and begin to cover more miles, the progress will be faster after a few months. Be patient. All-or-nothing programs are usually given up quickly. What you're after are regular habits that you will still have in a year or a decade. If you want to lose weight faster once you have been running for a while, start dieting as well.

Those who are severely overweight have more of a problem and have to be realistic in their expectations. If you need to lose fifty or a hundred pounds, you will not be able to do it as quickly or as casually as someone who needs to lose only ten. If you try, your attempt will be doomed to failure and frustration. Quite heavy people have the additional difficulty of not being able to burn up nearly as much weight with exercise because they are usually unable to go very far or fast. The best approach is to get a good diet (one that gives adequate nutrition) and to start on a standard walking or walking-and-jogging regimen. Don't overstress, but don't quit, either. The exercise will burn off pounds, albeit slowly, and more important, it will give you some positive motivation to keep going while maintaining your strength. Your starting point may be different, but you'll still see a lot of progress in three months and much more in six.

Body Types and All That

There has been a lot of deterministic nonsense written about body types—their origin in genetics, the womb, or early upbringing—and their inexorable influence on our lives. Similar mythologies exist about fat cells, heavy frames, and so on. It is of course true that much of our potential was determined long ago by various influences, but the statements that can be deduced accurately from those factors are usually both trite and obvious. It is not the obvious limits to our potential that are interesting but those that are novel or subtle. One that has been mooted by people who should know better is that there are body types that are determined early in life that fix not only adult build but personality as well.

The types are the ectomorph (lean and stringy), the mesomorph (a powerful, muscular build), and the endomorph (soft and plump), all supposedly deriving from the early development of the embryo. That the body types exist is obvious, but that they are fixed or connected in a predetermined way with particular person- ality types is a dubious proposition. We all know, of course, that some people gain weight more easily than others, and runners are equally familiar with the fact that some are naturally faster, re- spond to training more readily, and so on. What is interesting is how little we are predetermined. There are a host of classic en- domorphs who have turned themselves into lean and hungry run- ners. There are even powerfully built, mesomorphic types who have become world-class runners while retaining their muscula- ture.

No one completely understands the reasons why some people naturally stay lean while others put on weight readily, though we know a lot of contributing factors. There is evidence that fat cells developed in childhood readily store fat when it is available. Such cells are retained by the adult through life, but unless the person eats more food than he or she uses, the cells don't fill up. A lot of lean people simply are more active whatever they do, even when sitting in a chair, than those more prone to put on weight. Tastes in food, developed early in life, play a part, as do a host of other factors. Except for those with glandular abnormalities, however, there are no great mysteries about body build or weight control. Some of us have to work harder than others at it, but the formula is simple: if you use more than you eat, you will lose weight; if you eat more than you use, you will gain.

Build is also the source of a good deal of superstition and non- sense. Much is made of heavy bones and light ones or of small and large frames, yet two people of the same height will have skeletons that weigh nearly the same. The weight of the bones can account for a few pounds' difference at most. Musculature is a different mat- ter. Male body builders are the most extreme example; those in the championship category have little fat but a tremendous weight of muscle. Much of your build is controlled by the amount and type of exercise you engage in. Doing a lot of exercises requiring maximum strength will force the muscles to get larger. A lot of en- durance exercise uses calories but does not increase muscle bulk greatly. The structure of the muscles and tendons is the only really significant factor besides fat that accounts for weight differences be- tween those of the same height, despite the fact that people commonly explain differences of ten or fifteen pounds in weight as being the result of "heavy bones."

Unless you have designs on a world record or feel compelled to win at whatever you do, your body type, fat cells, or even the ratio of the types of muscle cells you possess is quite unimportant. What is important is to explore your own potential in a way that is satisfying and pleasurable. There is no one body type that enjoys running exclusively, though some will obviously succeed in it more readily than others. Some people are natural runners; they move into the state where running can be pleasurable far more easily and quickly than others. However, many such people never exploit their natural talent or are so competitive that they burn themselves out. People with less natural ability may have to work harder to reach the state where they really enjoy their running, but it can be all the more rewarding for being hard won. Similarly, if you start out without a lot of obvious running talent, then whatever level you reach can be satisfying, whether you jog at twelve minutes per mile or run a marathon at under six minutes a mile. The important things are the fun you have running and the achievement of your own goals. Along the way you may get a little extra satisfaction in proving that you don't have to fit someone's stereotype to be a runner.

Stretching and Warming Up

Warming up has been mentioned elsewhere as an important part of the daily workout. The reason is simple: when you start running, especially in the morning, your muscles tend to be somewhat stiff and do not function as well as after you have gotten moving. Part of this may be the result of the additional blood supply available after you have been working a little while; to improved lubrication, particularly of the joints; or to actual temperatures. Perhaps you simply relax more after you have been moving a few minutes. Whatever the reason, experience has shown that you are far more likely to get hurt if you try to start at maximum effort without a proper warm-up. Some people use the stretching routine to start warming up, some do calisthenics, and a lot of runners just start at a jog, an easy run, or a walk. The warm-up becomes increasingly important as you improve your condition. Start out at an easy pace, rather than beginning at top speed.

The novice should start thinking about stretching and begin to learn some stretching routines fairly early. (Stretching is discussed in detail in chapter 9.) People who are inactive tend to become rather inflexible, a condition that limits movement and makes one prone to injuries, because the muscles and joints are easily pulled beyond their atrophied limit of movement. Unfortunately, running does not improve the situation, nor do most strengthening exercises like weight lifting, isometrics, or push-ups. Running without stretching will slowly shorten a number of muscle groups, leaving you ripe for injury. Stretching properly will not only prevent this but will make you more flexible than you have been for a long time. You don't immediately have to start an extended stretching routine with your first run, but once you've established your running habit, start supplementing it with stretches. They can be done as part of your workout or at other times of the day when you have a few minutes. The flexibility they develop is another important component of good health.

Diet

The influence of caloric intake and weight on running have been discussed. Aside from this aspect of diet, runners are not much different from other people in their nutritional needs. It is just as well not to eat for a few hours before a run. During digestion, your stomach and intestines need a large share of the blood supply. During running, the leg muscles and cooling surface at the skin need the same blood. By giving your stomach time to get most of its work done before you run, conflicting demands are avoided. People are fairly adaptable in this respect, however—more than many nutritionists seem to understand. Many runners prefer to skip breakfast and sometimes lunch as well. Experiment a little to find out what is best for you.

Liquids are another matter. It is always best to drink too much rather than too little, particularly in hot weather. Have a glass of water or juice before you leave the house. Acclimatization to heat is discussed elsewhere, but here it must be noted that even if you

are trying to acclimatize, it is rarely a good idea to deprive yourself
of liquids. If you pass a fountain on your run, have a drink. When
you've progressed enough to do really long training runs, it is often
a good idea during hot weather to drop off a couple of water con-
tainers at strategic locations along the route. Loss of fluids is the
major limiting factor on performance in long runs. The advice that
one should avoid drinking during a workout is dangerous nonsense.
Nausea from ingesting water is unlikely, particularly if you drink a
moderate amount at a time. Drinks that replace the electrolytes
lost in sweating can be a good idea if you are perspiring a lot. The
standard commercially prepared ones are ERG, Body Punch, and
Gatorade. (Drinks are discussed in detail in chapter 12.) A lot of
runners prefer to dilute the Gatorade half and half with water. Salt
tablets are not a particularly good idea. You'll have to experiment
to find out what is best for you, but many runners prefer plain
water, especially during the run, and it is certainly adequate,
unless you are running more than a couple of hours.

Because of their concern with health, many runners experiment with different diets that purport to be the answer to all ills.
There is no question that the average American gets too many calories, too much fat, too much sugar, too much salt, and too many
additives, the effects of which on the body are inadequately understood. A balanced diet with reasonable quantities of protein and
lots of fresh vegetables, fruits, and whole grains takes care of most
of these problems, however.

There are good arguments for vegetarian diets and a host of
others, provided nutritional needs are met. (Proteins have to be
carefully balanced in a vegetarian diet to assure that amino acids
are available in correct proportions.) There is little reason to believe that such diets will improve your running performance, however, or that they are any more important for runners than for the
rest of the population. The superb performance and health of many
vegetarian athletes is a useful counterweight to the old view that
large quantities of steak, eggs, and dairy products are necessary.
Athletes need no more protein than anyone else, and excessive
quantities of meat, particularly meats high in fat content, probably
contribute to cardiovascular disease. You don't need more meat
just because you're running, and most of us would probably be
healthier if we ate less.

There is no evidence that large doses of vitamins are necessary or useful to runners or anyone else if they eat a normal balanced diet. About the only supplement that can be unreservedly recommended is iron for women, discussed more fully in chapter 6. Most vitamins won't do you any harm, as far as is known, the most important exception being vitamin A, which is poisonous in excessive doses. Large quantities of some vitamins may yet be demonstrated to have some value, but massive research hasn't turned up any yet. It also seems reasonable to believe that the human race has not evolved with a need for quantities of vitamins that were unobtainable in nature and could only be satisfied in the latter half of the twentieth century. Many athletes, however, are always in search of some magic potion that will give them a special edge. If you're worried about getting enough vitamins, standard multivitamin capsules with supplementary iron will serve as well as anything.

Two special diets commonly used by many runners on occasion are fasting and carbohydrate loading, both of which are discussed in Appendix I.

The Essential Principle of Moderation

Since the basic principle of training is that of stressing the body so that it will adapt and develop the ability to perform more work, the runner always takes the risk of falling into the mental trap of reasoning that if the hard week I put in last week did me this much good, then a little harder one this week should do even more. Obviously, at some point the body will break down instead of adapting. It will rarely break down without warning, but the runner in this mood is often quite adept at ignoring the danger signs. Remember, you have to learn to listen to what your body is telling you. More detail on injuries and prevention is included in chapter 10, but a few signs of overstress may be mentioned here. If they occur, slow down!

Signs of Overstress

1. Changes in your normal patterns of sleep, eating, or elimination. If you suddenly start needing two hours more sleep than you usually do or have difficulty sleep-

ing, for example, take a serious look at the amount and type of running you have been doing for the last week.

2. Irritability, difficulty in concentration, or other personality changes.
3. A resting pulse that is above normal, or overlong recovery times, indicated by pulse, breathing, or fatigue.
4. General listlessness or lack of enthusiasm about running or life in general.
5. Fever or general aches and pains, especially in the legs.
6. Injury, particularly pain that gets worse when you are running or that is getting worse from day to day.
7. Clumsiness in movement, or sloppiness in normal work.
8. Susceptibility to colds, headaches, flu, or indigestion.
9. Chronic thirst, rapid drop in weight, persistent dark- or amber-colored urine: all signs of dehydration. These are no causes for alarm after a long, hot run, but they should disappear after a few hours, never lasting from day to day.
10. Poor performance lasting more than a day or two. This may be reflected in increased times, the onset of heavy breathing at a lower level of effort than usual, or simply a feeling that you aren't up to par. Do not respond by concluding that you need to work harder.

The cure for overstress is obvious to anyone thinking rationally: *Slow down!* There is nothing wrong with taking a day off occasionally. Learn to distinguish between a weak will, which may need a bit of flogging, and a weak body, which should be pampered. Drop back to easy running until you feel better. Avoid sudden increases in mileage or speed, particularly sustained ones. If you want to start getting out twice a day, for instance, then add the second workout gradually. Do the second run on only one or two days the first week, two or three the second, and so on; or reduce the mileage of your first run when you add the second.

Aggressive runners are the most likely to run into these difficulties. Those who take a more casual, relaxed approach have the good sense to work toward their goals gradually. The principle of moderation is critical for everyone from the rankest beginner to the world-class runner. Feel for the correct amount of stress to train your body, but be sensitive to the signs that you are going too far. If you ignore the warning signs, you will have to pay the price of a long recuperation.

Smoking

It should go without saying that cigarettes and running don't mix. Running's primary effect on your body is to improve the strength and efficiency of the lungs, heart, and circulatory system; smoking's primary effect is to gradually destroy them. Running can be a useful tool for those who want to give up smoking, however. It makes the consequences fairly clear, because a smoker finds that he or she just can't breathe very well. A lot of people have managed to give up the habit after they started running. Running is also a useful rehabilitative exercise for reversing the effects of smoking. Probably no one who has smoked for ten or fifteen years will ever run a 2:10 marathon, but over a period of years many of the effects of smoking are reversible.

Many of the consequences of smoking have been repeated often enough to evoke a yawn by now. (Familiarity seems to breed contempt even for lingering and painful death.) Briefly, however, smoking causes lung cancer, cardiovascular disease, and emphysema. In the last disease the victim essentially suffocates to death over an extended period. Smoking also elevates the pulse rate some 15 to 30 percent. Because of the nicotine and cyanide that dissolve in the saliva, serious diseases of the digestive tract and the kidneys can also result, including cancer of the kidney. Pipe and cigar smokers who don't deliberately inhale reduce the damage to the lungs and heart somewhat, though the danger to the kidneys and the digestive tract is increased. Nonsmokers who get a lot of secondhand smoke from coworkers or spouses suffer the same effects as a person who smokes a quarter to half a pack a day. A few puffs of a cigarette—yours or someone else's—are enough to increase measurably the resistance in the lungs to the passage of air.

6/Women Running

The most exciting aspect of the current explosion in U.S. running is the participation by women and older runners. If a man out running on the roads used to be looked on with a raised eyebrow, a running woman was thought to be mad as a hatter. In competitive running, women were almost completely excluded, particularly from distance events, the ones for which they are best suited. Psychological barriers have been most important of all. Insofar as an accepted doctrine existed, it was that running was unfeminine, was dangerous, built unsightly muscles, and was certainly something that no "nice girl" would want to do.

In many parts of the country, things haven't really changed much, so there is still a lot of room for tough, individualistic women to educate society by getting out and running. Even in more enlightened areas, the increasing number of women runners has brought mixed blessings: in many urban areas favorite jogging paths have attracted some dangerous spectators. Still, progress has been incredible. Road races are now not only open to women but have women's categories, and even the Amateur Athletic Union (AAU), the umbrella organization for amateur athletics in the United States, has finally seen the light, though there is still not a wide enough range of distances recognized for national championships. Internationally, progress is being made more slowly, with the Olympic authorities and a number of European countries still marching resolutely back into the nineteenth century. In the face of the tremendous growth in women's running, however, things are bound to change soon.

Because of its very newness, women's running is one of the most exciting facets of the sport. If it has any equal, it is in the

The vast increase in the number of women running, particularly over long distances, is one of the most exciting features of the running movement.

parallel—often convergent—development of older runners. (A lot of the best women runners are middle-aged, perhaps the most prominent one being Miki Gorman, now in her forties, who has held the marathon women's record, won the New York Marathon, and won twice at Boston, with a pause in between to have a baby.) Both these movements are especially exciting for two related reasons, one being that no one knows what the possibilities are because we don't know how fast young women or old women or old men can run. Even more important is the fact that thousands of people who never had any positive athletic experiences before are suddenly discovering the joy of running and through it are discovering their own bodies and physical potential.

In the area of maximum potential, the men's and women's records in the marathon illustrate why women's running is so much more interesting. The men's record—2:08:33—was set by Derek Clayton of Australia in 1969. At the time of this writing it has stood for well over eight years. Even twenty-five years ago the record was only ten minutes slower. Although it would be rash to say that the men's limit is being approached, I wouldn't hold my breath waiting for the runner who breaks two hours to come along. In the women's marathon, on the other hand, the record has been broken a dozen times in the last decade, and there is no end in sight. In that time it has dropped more than thirty-seven minutes.

The struggles against sexism have resulted in some fine tales of heroines and villains. Probably the most publicized occurred after Kathrine Switzer of New York registered in the 1967 Boston Marathon as K. Switzer. Her boyfriend picked up her number and she started in the pack with all the other nuts, running from Hopkinton to Boston. When she was spotted by race promoter Jock Semple, however, he jumped off the official vehicle in a rage, assaulting K. Switzer in an attempt to tear off her number and purify the race as a strictly masculine trial. Fortunately, a rather large male runner who was trotting beside Kathy Switzer had the presence of mind to knock Semple flying off the course. Best of all, the whole incident was immortalized on film, so Jock Semple has had an opportunity to rue his lack of chivalry at leisure, and the all-male Boston Marathon was doomed.

Starting to run is not much different for a woman than for a man, once she overcomes any initial reticence she might have. The first few days and weeks are the hardest: getting the running habit, learning that it can be fun, finding a companion at the same level if she wants or needs one, and discovering her initial capacities. Women tend to run more naturally and with better style than men when they start, because they have fewer preconceptions about what proper running should look like and are less likely to try to go too fast at first. I remember inwardly groaning not long ago when a nonrunning male acquaintance announced proudly that he had "taught" his daughter to run. Her style was nearly perfect before, like that of most young girls, and the teaching most likely concentrated on making her look like a baseball player dashing for first base—up on the toes with arms pumping at full force.

Women run naturally, letting their arms move as they want to, neither letting the hands flop loosely nor holding them tight against the chest. The arms naturally counterbalance the movement of the legs, and they pump harder as one runs harder. The legs and feet should move straight ahead, in an easy and relaxed movement unless one is sprinting. There is very little difference among good runners between the style of women and men, less than the individual differences between members of the same sex. A woman's hips swing a little more because her pelvis is wider, but that's all.

Physical Differences and Their Implications for Runners

One of the more ridiculous vestiges of the tradition that women are the weaker sex has been the resistance in the sports establishment to allowing women to run in long-distance races. This is particularly ironic because women are better suited physiologically to running long distances than short ones, a view that was pressed for years by the great German training theorist Dr. Ernst van Aaken. Properly trained, women can easily run just as far as men, and there is some evidence that they may be able to do so more easily.

Given the physiological capacities of the sexes, it is difficult to conceive of a woman ever running the hundred-yard dash as fast as a male athlete of comparable ability, or reaching a four-minute mile. At longer distances, however, what will happen is anyone's guess. Personally, I think women will eventually run marathons as fast as men. Standards are partly a function of psychology, training methods, the level of competition, and the number of people competing. Women's marathoning is only a few years old, yet the winning times today in an important race like Boston or New York are comparable to those when the men's field was an equivalent size. In 1977, 141 women ran officially at Boston, and Miki Gorman ran 2:48:33 on a hot day. Back in 1951, when the size of the men's field was comparable and the temperature was more moderate, this time would have earned her fifteenth place. In 1952, another hot year, it would have been good for sixth. The world's record for men in April 1952 was 2:25:39, less than thirteen minutes faster than Jacqueline Hansen's current record of 2:38:19, yet it followed many more years of men's marathoning than women have yet had. Whether this reasoning is correct remains to be seen, but there is little doubt that women's records will continue to fall at a rapid rate for some time. Equally exciting is the fact that the chance of winning important races has not yet been narrowed in women's running to an elite group as much as in men's races.

The growth in competitive distance running has paralleled the enormous increase in running generally. These runners are passing a watering station in a fifteen-kilometer road race.

There are numerous physiological differences between men and women, some of which would appear to have important consequences for runners. Women generally have less powerful muscles, partly because of inborn differences between the sexes and partly because girls are not encouraged to use their muscles as much as boys during the developmental years. The skeletal structure supporting the muscles is also generally lighter in women, though there can be some training effect here. The wider, looser pelvic structure of women is a bit weaker in its ability to withstand large forces. All these factors, insofar as they may affect performance, will reduce women's times only in short events like sprints and hurdles. The apparently lower maximum oxygen-uptake levels of women would presumably reduce capacities in middle distances and perhaps lower possible times in long-distance runs. Women have a larger percentage of body fat than men, though this difference is reduced in trained runners. As a result, glycogen-storage capacity and available fluid reserves may be lower for a woman, and both these factors may play a role in distances over twenty miles. On the other hand, Dr. van Aaken and Dr. Joan Ullyot, a marathon runner and exercise physiologist, have suggested that women are better adapted to metabolizing fat for fuel and that since fat metabolism supplies the primary source of energy in the later stages of long runs, women may have a major advantage here. Furthermore, a critical factor in long-distance running may be the percentage of maximum oxygen uptake that can be sustained for long periods. There have been suggestions that women may be better able to maintain uptakes near their maximum for extended times. This, too, may give women some major advantages in distance races.

The fact is that no one really knows enough about physiology in distance racing to be able to answer many practical questions conclusively. Much theoretical evidence can be presented in favor of various training methods, for example, but none of it is conclusive. Not nearly enough research has been done. Much of it compares the effects of different training regimens on untrained men for relatively short periods of time, yet the results are then taken to apply to highly trained athletes running longer distances and engaging in prolonged training programs. So little research is available on women athletes, particularly distance runners, that no one really has any good answers. One can only speculate. It is women running who will eventually fill in the gaps in our knowledge.

Periods, Pregnancy, and Such

Most women who are already running regularly have no particular difficulty in continuing to run during any phase of their monthly cycles. Some feel they do not run quite as well, but this is of real concern only to serious competitors, some of whom have felt that they have run better during a period. Many women find that running their regular workouts reduces problems with cramps. Every woman has to experiment to find out what is true for her. Those who take diuretics (drugs that reduce retention of water) during some phases of their cycles to reduce bloating should be cautious about using these prior to long races or during heat training, since they may dangerously reduce the body's normal fluid reserves.

Iron deficiencies are common in women because of monthly blood loss and the inadequate supply of iron in the normal diet. There is some evidence that all runners may have increased needs for iron anyway, and because of the need for a maximum number of oxygen-carrying red blood cells, runners will certainly feel iron deficiencies more than inactive individuals. Regular use of some kind of iron supplement therefore seems advisable for women, particularly anyone who feels run down or experiences a decline in performance at levels of maximum effort. (Dr. Ullyot, in *Women's Running,* has pointed out that timed or delayed-release iron supplements are worthless, because iron absorption takes place early in the digestive tract, and a slow-release pill therefore insures that the iron will not be available where it can be used.)

The antiquated fears of male doctors about the incapacities of women in pregnancy seem to be gradually going out of vogue, particularly concerning activities with which the doctor is personally familiar. Skiing obstetricians worry about horseback riding, and horseback-riding obstetricians worry about skiing. This seems to be another good argument for finding doctors who run. Women might want to try to find female doctors who run, though this may be a difficult task. Most physicians are coming around to the view that a pregnant woman can continue to do whatever she is used to doing throughout most of her term. You may not want to follow the example of racers who have continued to run competitively well into pregnancy, but there is no reason not to continue regular running, unless some unusual complications occur. A woman cannot "jar the baby loose." The fetus is completely protected by the amniotic fluid that surrounds it until the sac breaks shortly before birth. The only logical restrictions seem to be on training much harder than one is used to or doing a lot of running that builds up a heavy oxygen debt. Running during pregnancy will probably assist in labor by maintaining good muscle tone and will certainly speed recovery after delivery.

Quite a few women have run their best races after having children. Miki Gorman ran up to a week before having her first child. She was running regularly again within a month after a delivery by Caesarean section and ran a marathon later the same year in less than three hours. Many other women racers have reached their peaks after having children.

Pregnancy is bound to slow women runners down a little, but there is no reason not to keep running aerobically.

Hecklers and Other Annoyances

Despite major changes in attitude during the last few years, women in some parts of the country are still made to feel pretty strange if they decide to start running. Most of this problem is psychological, of course—not nearly as many people will look askance as you think—but it is still real. The biggest problem for a lot of women, even more than men, is learning not to worry about what the neighbors think. The more out of shape one is, the more bothersome this may be. It's difficult to advise anyone else on this point; we each have to find our own answers to problems like this. It is often helpful, though, to develop a strong sense of self-righteousness. A woman can think about how much good she is doing herself and feel superior to all those people sitting in front of their television sets and eating Danish pastries. This holier-than-thou attitude does not have to be carried through the day, of course, but it may be useful while one is jogging around the block at six in the morning.

Both the problems just alluded to and the ones discussed in the next section can be greatly alleviated by a running companion. A spouse may be fine if he is at the same level. If he runs marathons at six-minute miles, however, he probably won't make a very good running mate until the wife has progressed a good deal on her own. It's important to run at a pace that is right for oneself, particularly at the beginning; by running with someone at a different level, one will either get worn out almost immediately or feel (correctly) that the other person isn't getting any exercise at all. Alternatively, one's companion will be circling all around doing intervals while you are just trying to keep going. It's demoralizing.

It is worth a lot of effort to any beginner to find someone else at about the same level to train with. Ask around among your friends. You may be surprised at the people who are interested in beginning a running program. It is important to find someone who is as serious as you are, so that you are encouraged rather than impeded by the association. If a friend doesn't work out, you may be able to find an organized program in your area. Or try putting up a note on the bulletin board at a local shop that sells running shoes. If you have problems of one kind or another getting out alone, a good running companion can be one of the most valuable assets you will ever find.

With a friend along, a woman will have little difficulty in shrugging off any snide comments or imagined disapproval. The obvious mental derangement of runners is a joke among many confirmed pounders of the pavement. With a companion, you're not just a nut, you're a subculture!

For some reason, women seem to get more advice on running style than men do, particularly from men who know nothing about running except that they did the hundred-yard dash in junior high school. Ignore it!

Self-Protection

One of the unfortunate side effects of the increase in the popularity of running has been that women runners are probably less safe today in many cities than they were a few years ago. Popular places for jogging in urban areas have attracted thugs and rapists. The problem is real and serious. One friend of mine was raped after being forced into a car at gunpoint. She was running with friends but had fallen somewhat behind the group. Several other friends and acquaintances have had near misses.

In most places this problem can probably be discounted. Fortunately, the probability of such an incident in most suburbs and rural areas is low enough to be ignored. Such incidents are possible anywhere, but they are sufficiently unlikely so that a woman does not have to spend her life worrying about them. Determining the borderline is necessarily subjective. If a woman is worried enough so that her running is spoiled, it doesn't matter what the objective risks are. They are real enough for her.

The greatest danger seems to be in parks in cities and college towns that joggers regularly frequent but that also provide plenty of lonely spots and a lot of opportunity for concealment. Thugs have become attracted to such places, and some of them even try to dress like runners. (Shoes are often a giveaway, once one learns to recognize standard brands. Nonrunners don't spend thirty or forty dollars on new Nikes or Adidas.) The worst situation seems to exist in parks that are open to automobile traffic, and the frequency of police patrols is also a factor.

The best solution in an area where assault is a real danger is to run with friends. This is particularly important when running at night. A faster runner can always run laps back and forth around a slower companion but should not get too far ahead. A dog of reasonable size can help insure a runner's safety. Even if the dog is a creampuff, it will probably discourage a potential assailant.

In dangerous cities, avoid running in places where there are lonely spots, particularly with good opportunities for concealment: bushes, dark alleys, vacant lots, and the like. Stick to well-lighted areas with lots of pedestrian traffic, particularly if you are alone after dark. Don't worry about a few stares; in the city at night they are preferable to dimly lighted parks, unfortunate as this fact is. If you have to run in the dark, the early morning hours are probably safer than the late night ones.

If you are running in a place where there is significant danger, pay attention to what is around you. Runners tend to slide off into their own mental worlds after hitting their pace during a long run. Stay alert instead. If you hear footsteps behind you, don't assume they belong to another runner. Look around and see.

If you run very much in places where assault is a serious hazard, or if the possibility disturbs your peace of mind, carry a weapon or some kind of device for attracting attention. In the former category, a small pressurized canister of Mace (a chemical compound that irritates the eyes, respiratory passages, and skin) is probably the best solution, although it is illegal in many localities. A similar device is Halt, a dog repellent in a small pressurized can, available from many bike shops. It is manufactured by Animal Repellents, Inc., Griffin, Georgia 30223. Anything that makes a lot of noise or light may be effective in frightening off a potential assailant, especially if you can use the distraction to sprint off. In the latter category are whistles and horns powered by small canisters of pressurized gas. Compact flare guns made for survivors of air crashes are also occasionally available in army-surplus stores.

PART 2

MAINLY FOR PRACTICING ADDICTS

7 / *Running Long*

This book is primarily about long-distance running. Since it is written for average runners and beginners rather than for championship athletes, most of its readers will run mainly for fitness, at least at the early stages of their running careers. And it is distance running that has the most to offer the fitness runner and jogger. Long distances build endurance, and under the influence of Arthur Lydiard and Ernst van Aaken, extensive distance work has become part of the normal training routine for runners who compete in races anywhere from eight hundred meters up.

Most important, however, are the pleasures of long-distance running. The intense physical and psychological joy experienced by so many runners is primarily a phenomenon of long aerobic runs, when the body swings along effortlessly through the countryside and all seems at peace. Hard, anaerobic running at shorter distances, whatever its rewards, is rarely an occasion for contemplative spiritual joys. It hurts too much.

If my own reasons for preferring distance running are mainly hedonistic, the rationale behind using it for training even middle-distance runners is more pragmatic. Van Aaken, Lydiard, and their disciples argue that competitive runners do not lack for speed, that speed is largely inborn. Once a person is in fair condition and has learned reasonable technique, it is maintained. Sprint speed can't be improved much by training. Rather, it is the inability to sustain that speed which slows the racer down, whether the race is the half mile or the marathon. It is stamina and endurance that are lacking. Running long distances at relatively slow speeds is therefore the base training for running all distances beyond sprints. Long-distance training has the additional advantages of helping control weight, generally toughening the athlete, and building the reserve

117

of strength necessary to sustain the competitive runner in hard
speed-training sessions later on.

Distance running at moderate aerobic paces has also been dis-
covered by many competitive runners who previously trained hard
at fast speeds through innumerable injuries, only to find that extended running at a more reasonable pace was not only more fun
but also improved their racing and reduced the number of their injuries or eliminated them altogether. Foremost among them have
been Ron Daws, Tom Osler, and Joe Henderson, editor of the
magazine *Runner's World,* author of a number of books, and coiner
of the conventional American term for this type of training, LSD
(for *long, slow distance*).

Pushing Up the Distance

For beginners, initial progress is likely to be marked by concentration on moving to more and more continuous jogging and
then to slow-paced running. A daily workout of forty-five to sixty
minutes should be a long enough session, and the novice will naturally go farther and farther during that same time period, as his or
her fitness improves. It is important not to try to press the rate of
increase too hard, however. Keep the overall workout aerobic,
without allowing yourself to coast too much. Breathing and pulse
can be used as gauges of whether you are exercising in the right
general range. If you're out of breath most of the time, you're
working too hard. If you aren't even breathing deeply, you're
being too easy on yourself. Keep your pulse above the threshold
rate. (Pulse rates are discussed on pages 88–92.)

The choice between working up to faster speeds and working
to greater distances is often posed in discussions on training. To
some extent, the relatively long sessions suggested here guide the
beginner toward increasing distance rather than speed. This is in-
tentional: distance training builds endurance (which provides the
surest base for developing speed), is ideal for cardiopulmonary conditioning, and helps the runner cut down body weight.

By the time the novice progresses to relatively slow but continuous running, at perhaps ten minutes per mile, he or she will be
covering 4.5–6 miles per day in the allotted time. This is a good
base, and if you are satisfied with the amount of work you are

The economical running style of these master runners is worth emulating. Note how their hands are carried low and relaxed; arm motion does not carry into the shoulders. Olympic gold medalist Frank Shorter leads Chicagoan Mike Slack in a fifteen-kilometer road race, but Slack later pulled ahead.

doing, don't hesitate to stay at this level for a long time. You will gradually become much more fit by maintaining this pace, your speed will probably slowly improve, and you will automatically gain some additional distance.

By this time, however, you may be interested in doing more work than simply jogging five miles a day or in improving at a faster rate than this seems to allow. Once you are comfortable at this pace, there are a number of variations you may want to try to stimulate your body to develop faster. Playing with your pace and stride was suggested as one of the things you should try when you feel comfortable with the distance of your normal workout. Although it is probably a poor idea to make pushing for speed an important part of your workout, speeding up parts of your runs is enjoyable and good training. Occasionally running a hilly course is another worthwhile endeavor, both in terms of interest and as a training tool.

The best direction to look for a greater challenge at this stage, however, is again toward increased distance. Try extending your runs occasionally, perhaps by doing a long run of a couple of hours one day of the weekend. Depending on the length and speed of your usual run, try going on a jaunt of eight, ten, or twelve miles in the country. Don't strive to run at top speed when you are first trying out a longer distance. Run at an easy, comfortable speed that you feel you can maintain for an extended period.

If you have been running shorter distances for some time, pushing up your mileage can be a new experiment with your abilities, not unlike the original one that you experienced when you started running.

Extending your distance can open up new running horizons. There are days when you will suddenly feel as though you were flying along, going fast and with relatively little effort after five or ten miles, at a point where you would usually begin to feel fatigue. On the good days, at least, the possibilities open like flowers, and visions of endless runs along backcountry trails, great loops from home, marathons, or even ultramarathons flit through your oxygen-starved brain. Lest you become overambitious, however, keep a rein on yourself when you begin to increase your distance well over what you have run before.

The general approach recommended in this book is to run long distances slowly as you increase the length of your runs. (As always, both *long* and *slowly* are relative terms, dependent on the experience and current capacities of the individual. A slow distance for some is ten miles at twelve minutes per mile; for others it is thirty miles at a seven-minute pace.) This is the safest and most painless way to increase the capacities of the body from the base running level to which it has already become adjusted. Even this pacing has certain pitfalls, however.

Cautions

When you begin to increase your distance, you are in a different position from the rank beginner. Whether you're working up to a marathon or trying to bring your average weekly mileage from twenty up to forty or to move from fifty to a hundred, you have already achieved a certain amount of competence. Your body has become accustomed to the stress of running, and it will absorb a fair amount of abuse before complaining too loudly.

As an intermediate runner, you have a greater capacity for hurting yourself than the neophyte, at least in those areas in which runners are typically vulnerable. You are, however, a lot less likely to have a heart attack. Indeed, you may have begun to consider yourself invulnerable to heart attacks, as many runners do. (No one is invulnerable, but you probably will have lowered the probability of suffering one.) In many less vital parts of the body, however, intermediate runners are far more capable of injuring themselves than are beginners. The archetypal running ailments are chronic symptoms of overstress in the muscles, tendons, and joints that are pressed to their capacities and beyond by tens of thousands of kicks and road shocks. A few of these injuries, particularly aching muscles and shin splints, may be experienced by beginners, but in the case of the novice, they are generally just the passing complaints of muscles being reawakened after long disuse.

The sort of injury that gets progressively worse is rarely experienced by the tyro, particularly if he or she follows the practice of long, slow workouts rather than short, fast ones. The reason is simple. The beginner's primary limitation is in aerobic capacity: he gets out of breath long before his knees begin to give out. And since lack of wind makes itself felt very quickly, the novice runner with a healthy heart usually can't overstress his body too much. There are plenty of exceptions, particularly among heavily built runners, but this is the typical pattern.

The situation is quite different once you can comfortably run several miles a day. Whether it takes you a year to reach this stage or whether you start there, you will discover that you have far greater reserves that can be tapped by an act of will. You can keep yourself going by drawing on the reservoir of conditioning that you have built up. You can probably go out and run three times the distance you normally cover in a single session—without reducing your speed appreciably. You could also probably double your weekly mileage immediately. Unfortunately, by suddenly increasing the amount of stress you are placing on your body by this much, you tend to break it down rather than make it stronger. The danger that your greater endurance carries with it is the possibility of pushing your system far beyond its adaptive limits. Your aerobic capacity is also probably a good deal greater than the capacity of your legs to keep up.

In terms of regular running, the best safety rule is to avoid increasing your mileage more than 10 percent a week. This is intended as an average figure. If you go out one Sunday and do a twenty-mile run instead of your usual seven, of course it will increase your weekly total a lot, but it will probably do you good, provided you don't try to follow it up by lengthening your daily run by a couple of miles for each of the next six days and then doing another twenty. Follow the first long run with a couple of easy days instead, and don't try to bring up your daily runs until your body has had a chance to adjust. If, for example, you have decided you want to double your regular weekly mileage, plan to take seven or eight weeks at a minimum to do it. If you are already putting in relatively high mileages, you may need to take even longer. The 10-percent figure is one that is meant to provide a guideline for a reasonable maximum figure to use as a goal. It is a modest enough increase to give your body time to tell you whether or not it is adjusting. You must be alert to signs of overstress and cut back if they should appear.

The most important progress for the intermediate runner is learning to run longer distances. Distance brings certain hazards with it, however, especially if the runner pushes for speed at the same time.

There is generally less danger of injury from a single long run than from radically increasing your weekly mileage, but it is important to realize that long, fast runs at the limit of your capacity tend to drain your reserves rather than build them. Racing, particularly over long distances, generally requires a recovery period of easy running if it is done with maximum effort. The same principle applies to any long runs that are done as though they were races. Unless your purpose is to test yourself and you intend to allow a recovery period during the next week, do your long runs at speeds that are comfortable for you. When they are done in this way, you'll probably still feel the effort the following day, but your body should bounce right back.

It is important to be on the lookout for subtle symptoms of overstress when you are increasing mileage. Look over the list at the end of chapter 5 and keep it in mind. Be wary of sore tendons and muscles that are slowly getting worse day by day. It is easy to tell yourself that they are staying the same, until one day you find you can't even walk. A long, hard run may tax your reserves considerably without really making you feel bad. The signs of strain may be in lack of resilience rather than in overt aches or fatigue.

How Long?

There are some rules of thumb for deciding how much you need to run each week in order to reach particular goals. Ultramarathoner Ken Young proposed the theory that during an all-out push like a race, a runner could run 5 percent of the total training mileage done in the preceding two months before reaching the collapse point. When Young talks about the collapse point, he is referring to the radical slowing that a seasoned distance runner experiences in very long races. This phenomenon, accompanied by an assortment of discomforts that beggar description, is commonly referred to as "hitting the wall"—the runner feels as though he is continuing on willpower alone. (Dr. Joan Ullyot claims that women runners may not experience this barrier.)

The two-month mileage figure is important, because there is a long lag before the effect of increased mileages is felt. Thus, if you have suddenly started running much more mileage in the last couple of weeks, you won't be able to run farther in a stint tomorrow than you could have before the change. In fact, you could probably run less. If your training has been consistent, however, you should be able to run a distance equal to three times your average daily mileage, figured over a seven-day week. Though there are some qualifications needed, a large number of runners have found that Young's formula works fairly well.

Suppose, for example, that during the last few months the longest you have run in a consecutive sixty days is 340 miles. Dividing 340 by 20 gives you a collapse point of 17 miles. This means that on a good day, with everything working in your favor, you would be able to run 17 miles in a race before you slow down radically. If you have to fight the wind, run a hillier course than you are accustomed to, pace yourself incorrectly, or just have a poor day, you will slow down even earlier. (Three times the daily average of 5⅔ miles yields the same collapse figure of 17 miles.) Thus, if you wanted to train to run a marathon without hitting the wall, you would need to run at least 524 miles (20 times 26.2) during a two-month period preceding the race, an average of a little under 9 miles a day.

This same average can be used to give you a good idea of the length of long training runs you might want to take. Suppose you have been running regularly for some time, doing about 5 miles a day, five days a week. Your weekly mileage is then 25, and the daily average over the whole week is a little over 3.5. You might expect your collapse point to be at about 10.5 miles. Ten miles would then make a good distance for a long run, but for training you should run it at an easy pace. Such extended runs help teach the body to function at a good level of effort for long periods. They also accustom you to such distances. If you are training for a race or a hard-effort run, they have the immense psychological advantage of confirming your ability to handle the distance, without the strain of doing it at full speed.

Even if you are running at an easy rate, however, you shouldn't run much farther than your regular distance too often. One run a week that is more than twice your daily average is enough.

How Fast?

It is hard to overemphasize the importance to the intermediate runner of adding distance at slow to moderate paces. Most of your distance running should be well within your aerobic capacity. By this time, of course, striding out some of the time, maintaining your pace on hills, and making occasional spurts of varying distance and intensity are all fun and are good training. You should not press the limits of your speed for long distances very often, however. Trying to increase distance and speed at the same time is the formula for a breakdown.

Even if your goal is racing, the same advice applies to your distance work. In fact, it may apply even more. If you want to race immediately and to do a lot of speed work, stick to the weekly mileages you are already doing. If you're still trying to build up basic endurance and you want to increase your mileage, stick to that objective and run any races you participate in as training runs. Keep the pace fairly comfortable.

Road Running

As you extend your mileage, you are bound to do a lot of running on the roads. Precautions in dealing with traffic have already been outlined (chapter 2), but it is important to remind yourself of the dangers that automobiles pose. It is astoundingly easy to slip off into another world of consciousness while you are running along a country road, and this detachment from your surroundings leaves you vulnerable to any careless driver who may come along. It is also commonplace for runners to become overconfident in traffic, relying too heavily both on their own speed and on the drivers' competence. Strive to avoid these traps, particularly if you are running a lot of miles on the roads.

Remember that when you are running, you are completely at the mercy of the drivers around you. If a car coming in the opposite direction suddenly swerves, you are in for a nasty collision, even if it is going at a relatively slow speed. If it is going fast, you'll probably be killed. You do not have the protection that you do when you are driving. Furthermore, the road runner has a lot of ex-

Pushing up the distance often means long runs on country roads.

posure time. Putting in a couple of hours a day, year in and year out, is fairly common. Much of the risk of an accident is simply a function of this time factor; if you run twice as long, you have twice the risk. That is why insurance companies raise drivers' rates when they drive more miles in a year. You can't afford to increase even a little the probability of getting hit.

Try to avoid running too much on roads with a pronounced crown, unless you can find a level section along the shoulder much of the time or a stretch where the traffic is so light that you can run the center line. Running along pavement that is angled to one side can cause a number of leg problems if you are covering a lot of miles on it. The problem can be alleviated somewhat by running half the time on the right-hand side of the road, but this may be unsafe unless the road is quite wide or the traffic is light.

Trail Running

If you are lucky, you may have a good trail system within a reasonable distance of your home that can be used for running, at least when the weather permits. Trail surfaces vary a great deal, ranging from the ideal resilience and smoothness of forest humus and of some artificially surfaced trails to the rough and hazardous characteristics of many mountain trails.

Runners' tastes differ almost as much as trails. Nearly anyone is happy to run on woodland trails that are perfectly smooth with just a slight give, but people have different feelings about trails that are hilly, strewn with rocks and obstacles, or both. Aside from the rare exceptions, running on trails is slower than running on pavement. Rough trails pose a real danger that the runner may turn an ankle or twist a knee, particularly if he or she doesn't pay constant attention to footing. On the other hand, with proper running technique trails may pose less of a danger of chronic injuries associated with perpetual banging on pavement at the same gait and often on an angled surface.

Aesthetic considerations make me a confirmed trail runner. During the season when the trails in my area are in good condition, I take to the roads only reluctantly. The varied pace needed for handling the changing gradients of the mountain trails near my home is good training and far more interesting than road running to me. The beauty of the surroundings is incomparable. If I run more of a risk of breaking an ankle on the trails, I run far less of a risk of being hit by a car going sixty miles per hour. In the end, however, it is the smell of the pines, the color of the early morning sun on the rock, and the chattering of squirrels that bring me back to the trails again and again.

There are some tricks to trail running that anyone who runs them very much should learn. If the trails where you live are rough, pick shoes that allow stable foot placement, even on undulating ground. Running shoes are not generally made to hold the foot against strong lateral forces, as tennis shoes are. Still, some running shoes are better than others in this respect. Foot placements on rough trails are often on sidehills so that a lateral force is exerted by the foot. Many training shoes are quite dangerous both because they have thick soles, bringing the foot high off the ground so that there is a greater tendency to roll when the shoe lands at an angle, and because they combine this height with lack of support against sideways motion. In general, less padding is necessary for trail running, particularly when your feet have become accustomed to it. Running shoes with a lower, more stable profile can often be worn comfortably and more safely. Try to be sensible about the time that you run on trails. Except on those rare trails that are perfectly smooth, it is dangerous to run in the dark or even in twilight. It is too easy to make a misstep. Ice can be very dangerous, and snow that conceals the footing is risky. Rain usually only makes things messy.

Hilly trails are excellent for leg strength, wind, and hill technique. They won't do much for your speed, of course. Those who are trying to learn racing technique may want to run down hills at full speed, because practice can greatly improve performance. Unless you have this purpose in mind, however, I would recommend that you jog the downhill sections, or at least run them slowly most of the time. Downhill running is hard on the knees, and the risk of turning an ankle is greater if you run downhill fast.

Annoyances and Complaints

Several minor imbalances may occur in the body as a result of long runs, particularly if you go a little farther than your capacity. These should cause no real problems, provided you don't overtax yourself frequently. They can be alarming if you don't expect them, however, aside from whatever annoyance they cause in themselves.

You should expect that your legs will begin to feel like lead if you are pushing beyond your comfortable capacity, for that day at least. Prickly sensations and numbness are also possible. Any parts of your legs that have been injured or are vulnerable may give you a little trouble, and some aches and pains may persist for a day or two after a really long run. They should improve rapidly, rather than getting worse or becoming chronic, however.

Stiffness and aching in the upper back and shoulders may occur if you are running much farther than you are used to. Such tightness coming on early in the run indicates that you are tense. Stretching, shaking the arms around while trying to relax the muscles, and letting them bob limply at your sides while you are running may help. You may experience tingling or numbness in the fingers, hands, or arms after a long run. This results simply from the blood being shunted to the legs, where it is most needed. Such numbness is of no consequence in these circumstances. But numbness or pain associated with running fast, going up hills, or similar periods of higher stress could indicate a heart problem and should prompt you to visit the doctor.

Minor dehydration will make you thirsty, of course. Urine production will be reduced and the urine will be amber colored. Such low-level dehydration is normal when you are running on warm days, particularly in humid weather. Serious dehydration and heat effects (discussed in chapter 4 and in the next three chapters) can be very serious, however. Dizziness, weakness, chills, the cessation of sweating, or loss of the sensation of heat during the run are all symptoms of heat injury. Slow down and get to water and shade. After the run, a couple of hours of drinking should restore the body to normal. Drink as much as you comfortably can if you think you have become dehydrated. It isn't usually necessary to worry about exact quantities, but if you want to know how much you need to take in to restore the fluids you have lost, remember that a pint of water weighs about a pound. If your weight is six pounds off when you come in from a run, you'll have to drink about three quarts of liquid to replace what you lost. Some of this liquid should be fruit juice or a prepared electrolyte replacement drink that will restore salts lost in perspiration. A loss of weight or the passing of amber-colored urine persisting to the following day indicates chronic dehydration.

Stitches are sharp pains in the sides of the waist area, to which some runners are more vulnerable than others. Most people have experienced them while running after a heavy meal. They seem to be associated with breathing that expands only the chest and not the abdomen, probably because holding the abdomen rigid results in impairing circulation in the diaphragm. Thus, stitches are most common when the stomach is full and in downhill running, when the abdomen tends to be held rigid. With well-conditioned runners, learning to "belly breathe," expanding the stomach when breathing rather than raising the chest, usually makes one less subject to stitches. Creating some resistance in the mouth or throat while exhaling may also help rid you of a stitch. Beginners and runners training at higher speeds than they are used to will also tend to have problems, because the diaphragm is working harder than it is used to. Slow down until the stitch disappears.

8/
Exercise and Flexibility for the Habitual Runner

Running by itself is not the ideal exercise. It has major advantages as a method of achieving and retaining fitness, but like everything else in life, it is less than perfect. Those who run on a regular basis over a long period are likely to develop some problems that can be prevented by a few supplementary exercises and stretches.

The deficiencies of running fall into two or three main categories, depending on one's point of view. The most important is probably the fact that the muscles used in running gradually tend to shorten and become less flexible over the months and years unless something is done to counteract the process. This problem is compounded by the fact that because of their normal habits most Americans have rather tight and inflexible muscles anyway. Such tight muscles restrict the body's range of movement, so they are undesirable in themselves. In addition, as they become tighter and tighter, they are like guitar strings put under more and more tension to raise their pitch. Sooner or later, something will give. Either the muscle itself will be torn, or it will tear loose the attachment at one end. This may occur suddenly, as when a guitar string breaks or the bridge is torn loose, or it may occur slowly, like the gradual distortion and warping of the neck or sounding board of the instrument.

The solution to these problems of tightening muscles is quite simple: you have to stretch them out regularly to counteract the shortening tendency. Even a modest amount of stretching every day prevents both the tightening and the injuries it can cause. It also makes you more flexible and supple.

A second problem for some runners is the development of muscle imbalances, which can also cause both sudden and chronic injuries. The body includes many paired muscle groups; one half of each pair moves some part of the body one way, and the other opposing half pulls it in the reverse direction. Development of one muscle or group far more than its opposite can result in difficulties. Some of the troublesome muscles that are left undeveloped by distance running are the abdominal muscles, the quadriceps (the front muscles of the thighs), and the muscles on the front of the lower leg. Exercises designed to strengthen these muscles will prevent injuries caused by imbalance.

Some would also consider running an imperfect exercise because it fails to develop the upper body. Distance running does not even develop much power in the legs, despite their tremendous endurance. Such critics argue that these capacities should be improved through specific exercises, even though no particular problems are caused by these deficiencies. Certainly, if you are training for other sports that require muscular strength in particular areas of

Without complementary stretching and exercises, running tightens some muscle groups and permits others to remain too weak.

the body, you may want to do supplementary exercises to strengthen appropriate muscle groups. A cross-country ski racer, for example, might want to do arm exercises. Some theorists of running, notably the great Australian coach Percy Cerutty, have maintained that upper-body strength is important even for efficient running. Cerutty and others advocate the use of weight training, push-ups, chin-ups, and other resistance exercises to strengthen the torso and arms.

The runner can take any number of approaches to stretching and exercising, depending on individual needs, interest, time, and energy. From the point of view of overall fitness, the emphasis probably should be on running. Cardiopulmonary fitness remains the basic, most important element of conditioning of the body, and the beginning or intermediate runner is likely to have enough to do and think about managing his or her daily runs without adding a daily hour of stretches and calisthenics. But even runners who are not particularly interested in extensive stretching and exercise routines should get into the habit of practicing a small group of them, to prevent the most common runners' injuries and to maintain reasonable flexibility, muscle tone, and balance in the abdomen and legs.

Later in this chapter there is a list of the types of exercise and stretching that should be performed regularly by the habitual runner, together with some specific stretches and exercises that serve the purpose. The particular ones listed here are not necessarily superior to others that serve the same functions. The important thing is to stretch regularly those muscles that tend to tighten up in running and to do some exercises for the abdominal muscles and those along the front of the leg.

Many experienced runners, particularly those who have suffered injuries in the past that are attributable to lack of flexibility, may want to work out a more elaborate and better developed stretching and exercise program. Some suggestions are included to explore the methods that can be used.

Routines

As with running itself, the key to gaining benefits from stretching and exercising is establishing the routine of doing them regularly. Those who decide to try out a disciplined yoga sequence or a similarly ambitious stretching or exercise routine will have to find time during the day when they can carry these out. If you are content with a more rudimentary approach, however, at least for the present, there are a number of ways that you can work into your daily routine the most important stretches and exercises, many of which require almost no time at all.

One of the most popular sequences is a series of stretches and exercises before or after running, or both. In the morning, for example, you might get up, do a few bent-leg sit-ups, get dressed for running, and then do a series of stretches before starting out, perhaps while waiting for your running partner. You might follow the run with a few more stretches before heading for the shower. Other exercises can be worked in during the day.

Provided you do get into the habit of doing the needed stretching and exercising, however, it doesn't matter too much when you do them. Prerun stretching is helpful for some, particularly those running early in the morning, but if you do your stretching some other time and don't start running too fast, it probably does not alter the effect. If your running schedule is tight or if you find it hard to get up any earlier than you absolutely have to before a morning run, you may prefer to postpone your stretching. From a practical point of view, nearly all the necessary stretches and exercises for runners can easily be squeezed into the day during spare moments. (An exception should be made if you are having trouble with tightness or injury in a specific place, in which case it should be carefully stretched before running.)

Personally, I recommend that you try to do some bent-leg sit-ups either before or after the run, simply because these raise a bit of sweat, and it's nice to have a shower afterward. The other exercises mentioned here, however, together with all the stretches, can be done at virtually any free moment of the day, and they can yield the bonus of helping you to relax in the middle of the day.

Basic Exercises and Stretches

Abdominal strength is important for general good health. Weak abdominal muscles allow the stomach to sag out, tend to encourage bad posture, and often result in fatigue and back pain. The classic abdominal exercise, the sit-up, is hard for a lot of people to perform. During much of the motion the exercise actually stresses the hip flexor muscles rather than the abdominals; the abdominals themselves are active only in the first part of the sit-up. Bent-leg sit-ups, like those described later in this chapter, or similar exercises, are easier for most people to perform and more effective in strengthening the abdominals. Some type of exercise for these muscles should be included in the runner's routine.

The muscle at the front of the thigh, the quadriceps, often is relatively weak compared with the hamstring at the back after thousands of miles of running. Among other difficulties, this imbalance can result in knee pain. The main function of the quadriceps is to pull the lower leg forward from a bent to a straight position, so any exercise that involves straightening the leg against resistance will strengthen the quadriceps. Typical ones are sitting on the edge of a table and lifting a weight suspended from the foot or doing a similar lift with a weighted boot on. You can also straighten one leg from the bent-knee position while pushing back against the toe with the heel of the other foot. Weight rooms have special fixtures for lifting weights with the lower leg.

The muscles that run along the front of the lower leg tend to be much less developed than the calf muscles behind. Weakness in these "antigravity muscles" is one cause of shin splints. There are various complicated exercises to strengthen these muscles, but the simplest is to pull your toes up from a full extended position against resistance from above by the other foot. You can do this anywhere during an odd moment—sitting in the bus, watching television, lying in bed, or sitting at a desk typing.

Stretching the calf muscles and the Achilles tendons may be the most important single routine. Achilles problems are among the most common of runners' injuries, and most can be prevented by regular stretching. Simply leaning against the wall while resting your weight on one straight leg and letting the body lean forward enough to stretch the calf thoroughly does the job, though there are other good stretches with the same function.

Stretching is nearly as important for the hamstring as for the Achilles. The hamstring is the powerful muscle at the back of the thigh that drives the runner forward. Pulled hamstrings can strike any runner, but sprinters, hurdlers, and distance people doing speed work are the most common victims. Toe touching is a traditional hamstring stretch, but it is less effective than other stretches for many people. Several good hamstring stretches are shown in the illustrations that follow. Any one or a combination of them will do the job.

Stretching the back is important for general health and comfort. A stiff back leads to awkward movement and often causes tightening and pain during a long run. Many movements stretch the back well, and you can easily devise your own. Variations of the yoga plow position (see the illustration on page 138) are particularly good, since the weight of the legs helps one to stretch. Finish off by bending backward either from a standing position or by lying on the stomach and pushing the upper body up with the arms while keeping the thighs flat on the floor.

Stretching the muscles of the front of the leg helps to promote general flexibility and prevent injuries like shin splints. A couple of typical stretches for the ankle, the anterior tibial muscles, and the quadriceps are shown in the illustrations.

Foot and ankle exercises and stretching help to strengthen the many small muscles in this part of the body. Some possibilities are illustrated, but there are many others you can devise. Picking up objects with the toes, stretching in every possible direction, and forcefully flexing the feet and toes both when you are sitting and standing help prevent a host of running injuries.

Stretching Principles

Stretching is simplicity itself, once you learn how. The methods that most of us have been taught, as a part of calisthenics routines, are not very good. Bouncing and stretching violently do not work well. They invite injury by stretching muscles too far and too fast. They are ineffective because they induce a bounce-back reflex from the muscle being stretched. This elastic return is automatic and can't be controlled voluntarily.

The proper way to stretch any muscle is to extend it slowly until you can feel a strong tension in the muscle. Then hold the stretch and concentrate on relaxing the muscles being stretched. After a little while, if the muscle lengthens and feels comfortable, extend the stretch a bit more. Don't try to overdo things. If the

SPECIFIC STRETCHES AND EXERCISES

Any of the bent-leg sit-up exercises are good for strengthening the abdominal muscles. This is the one I like. Lie on your back, hands behind the head. Raise your head, shoulders, and arms and touch one elbow to the opposite knee, approximately over your waistline. Lie flat again and then touch the opposite elbow to the other knee. Repeat until your abdominal muscles feel stressed but not strained. This will seem easy at first, but if you can do a hundred repetitions, you have very strong stomach muscles!

The quadriceps, or front muscle of the thigh, can be strengthened by any exercise requiring the foot and lower leg to be straightened against resistance. Here, two weights tied together with a piece of one-inch nylon webbing are looped over the foot and raised with the leg. The exercise is then repeated with the other leg. The opposite leg could also be used to provide the resistance.

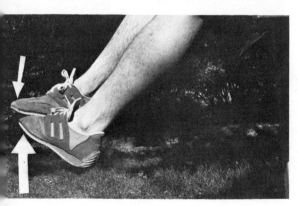

The muscles on the front of the lower leg can easily be strengthened by pulling the toes of one foot up against the resistance of the other foot. Move the foot being exercised through its whole range of motion so that the muscles will be strengthened in all positions. Then reverse the feet and repeat.

The heel cord and Achilles tendon are most easily stretched by leaning against something while keeping one leg straight with the sole of the foot flat on the ground. Stretch one leg at a time. The ankle should be twisted slightly out to stretch the tendon, but it is a good idea to stretch with the foot in several different positions to ensure that all the muscles and tendons at the back of the calf are stretched.

A very simple hamstring stretch: step forward with one leg, toe pointed straight ahead, and lean forward toward the knee, keeping the legs straight. The position of the arms is not important. You should feel the stretch at the back of your leg, a little above the knee. You should eventually be able to touch your chin to your knee. Repeat with the other leg.

A variation is to prop the leg being stretched up against a table or other support.

Another good hamstring stretch, which twists the trunk and neck, too. Spread the legs, with the toes of the leg to be stretched pointing straight to the side. Hold your arms straight out to the sides. Keeping your knees straight, turn your trunk and lean over to the side of the leg being stretched, sliding your hand down your leg as far as you comfortably can. If you can reach, try to put your palm flat on the ground. Look up at the opposite thumb. Repeat on the opposite side.

The plow is a good position for stretching the back, neck, and hamstrings. Since the weight of the legs and hips aids the stretch, be very careful to move *slowly*. Throwing your legs violently over your head could result in a nasty strain. Lie on your back on a soft but firm surface and move your legs back over your head. Don't worry about straightening them at first. Find the farthest position you can comfortably hold. Stretch as far as you can without straining.

One easy way to stretch the quadrilaterals and shin muscles is to stand using a support, reach one leg behind you, and grab it with the hand. Pull up with your hand and push the leg back until you feel the muscles in the front of the thigh stretch; then hold. Repeat with the other leg.

An even better stretch for the quadrilaterals, which also stretches the back, ankles, and shin muscles, is done by first kneeling with the feet pointed back and just outside the hips. Rest your hands behind you at first and let your body back slowly. Since the weight of the body is being used and there is leverage on the knees, lean back slowly and carefully until you feel the muscles in the front of the thighs stretch. Some people will be able to lie all the way back on the ground, whereas others will be able to lean back only a little.

Ankle and foot stretches can be done whenever you have a few spare minutes. Just stretch and twist your feet in every direction you can think of, both in the air and when you are standing. Picking up objects with the toes is good practice, or gathering up a towel using the toes. Try picking up a pencil with your toes and writing. With practice it can be done—with both feet!

Remember that with all these stretches the important object is not to reach a specific goal but to stretch regularly the muscles and tendons. You may easily be able to stretch farther than the positions shown, which are average ones for a fairly tight person. You may not be able to approach them at first. Most likely some will be easy and others impossible. Stretch slowly until you feel a pull—then hold. Relax in the position until the muscle loosens, and stretch a little more. Never strain!

muscle, joint, or tendon hurts, back off a little. The best effects are gained from consistency and regularity. Trying too hard will simply cause an injury. Be particularly cautious in doing any stretches in which the position gives you leverage on one part of the body, especially a joint, or where gravity assists the stretch by pulling on a large percentage of the body's weight.

Stretching should feel good! If it isn't pleasant, you are trying to push things and you are likely to hurt yourself. Do everything slowly, and don't strain. Remember, *don't bounce!* The typical toe-touching routine is an example of poor stretching technique. Relaxation is the key to achieving a good stretch. Pull the muscle out until you feel the tension, hold, and relax. Then stretch some more. Don't continue beyond the limits of comfort. You will be able both to stretch farther and to hold the stretches longer as the days and weeks go by.

Beyond the Basics

Runners who want to stretch or perform resistance exercises beyond the basic level presented here may want to investigate some other sources. Traditional calisthenics programs can be found in a wide variety of places, though the reader is likely to know enough to progress without much difficulty. Push-ups, pull-ups, and dips will develop most of the muscles of the upper body. (A dip, traditionally done between parallel bars, consists of supporting the weight of the body with the hands on two supports at about shoulder width, lowering oneself until the elbows are at right angles, and raising the weight of the body until the arms are straight again. Two chair backs or similar supports can be used if the knees are kept bent.)

One good general exercise routine is the Royal Canadian Air Force series, which is widely available in an inexpensive booklet. Those interested in weight training may want to look at the *Complete Weight Training Book*, by Bill Reynolds.

For flexibility, the traditional Indian discipline of yoga is unquestionably the best developed, most efficient, and soundest approach for anyone serious enough to pursue it. All the techniques now used in the United States for stretching are derived from yoga, and much of what has been learned about injury prevention in running and many other sports is directly attributable to the increased interest in yoga during the last few years.

If you are interested in studying the yoga postures, whether as a purely physical discipline or with some attention to the cultural background in which it was developed, the best book available is B. K. S. Iyengar's *Light on Yoga*. Following the courses outlined by Iyengar will take you as far as you want to go. This is a concentrated and uncompromising book; the sequences are extremely well thought out and will reward anyone who follows them.

For those who do not want to expend the mental and physical effort involved in pursuing yoga, there is a fine book called *Stretching*, by Bob Anderson, which adapts many yoga techniques for easy assimilation. It is an easygoing and enjoyable book as well.

Publication data on all these books are included in the appendix.

9 / Injuries

There are four primary causes of injuries to runners: overstressing the body, imbalanced training, structural problems in the body (particularly in the feet), and accidents. Many injuries are caused by some combination of the four. Accidents, for instance, are most likely to occur when the athlete is tired or already weakened by other injuries. In fact, of the four, accidents are by far the least frequent cause.

There is food for thought in the fact that serious, competition-oriented runners are more likely to suffer injuries than more casual, fitness-directed ones. Racers spend a lot of time talking about their injuries, sometimes to the point of absurdity. If you go to the starting line of a major race and stand around listening, by closing your eyes you could easily convince yourself that you were in the convalescent ward of the local hospital rather than among some of the fittest people in the country. Everyone is likely to be saying that they haven't gotten much mileage in lately because of an Achilles problem or a heel spur or sciatica. Then, of course, they'll all take off at the gun doing five-minute miles, and you can spend the rest of the race eating their dust and wishing a few injuries on them that will really slow them down.

A lot of running-injury chatter is simply shoptalk, hypochondria, a way of releasing tension before a race, or a kind of one-upmanship. (Joe can't lose when touting his torn hamstring. If he comes in first, he has done it in spite of his handicap. If he comes in thirtieth, he's made a magnificent showing, considering the fact that he had no business running at all.) The number of runners who really do suffer injuries is alarming, however. Many world-class runners spend half their time battling injuries.

Running injuries can be extremely frustrating and intractable. Runners are fortunate, compared with participants in some other sports, because they are rarely subject to broken bones, severe sprains, and dislocations. Except for occasional encounters with automobiles, a sprained ankle or a broken bone in the foot is usually the worst traumatic injury the runner ever suffers, and even these are unlikely. (A traumatic injury is one produced by a violent, physical force, such as a wound or broken arm.) The overuse injuries that plague runners, however, can slowly cripple the athlete, sap the energy and enjoyment from training, and drive him or her to distraction trying to get over it.

Because of the multiplicity of causes, it is often hard to decide on the remedy for a runner's problem. Many doctors are not oriented toward athletic injuries, and the frustrated runner visiting one of these is often brushed off, given bad advice, or talked into an unnecessary operation. This situation is improving, but we still have a long way to go. Runners often tend to ignore symptoms until they have become really serious or try to "run through the pain." The latter usually results in running into a lot more pain.

One of the most frustrating experiences of the injured runner is to keep developing the same problem, no matter what remedies are tried. Injuries that are more than transient incidents have underlying causes, and until those causes are uncovered and corrected, the problem keeps returning. This is particularly true of those injuries that result from imbalanced training or structural problems.

Overstress, the Primary Cause

Most runners' injuries follow directly from the fact that runners are not always too smart. We all know that overtraining will result in injuries—if someone else does it. We, of course, never overtrain.

Very few overstress injuries come about suddenly; most give plenty of advance warning. If you heed the warning within a reasonable period of time, no serious injury results. However, if you let things go, either because you assume that the pain will go away or because you don't realize that it is getting worse or for some other misguided reason, you have a good chance of developing a serious chronic injury. Problems around the heel and the Achilles tendon are typical examples of injuries that nearly always take a long time to become serious but that can become quite intractable if they are left to develop for a while.

Overtraining can manifest itself in many ways. (Some of the general warnings to look out for were listed on pages 101–2.) Briefly, you should be alerted by significant changes in eating, drinking, sleeping, or elimination habits. Be especially wary if you feel listless, tired, irritable, or just not up to par. Aching and tired legs before you run indicate that the workout the day before was too hard. Stressing the whole body beyond its limits can leave you ripe for injuries of various sorts and will lower your resistance to general ills like colds, flu, mononucleosis, strep throat, and intestinal bugs.

Whether or not such signs of general overstress manifest themselves, if you are going too hard or too fast, the weakest link in your body will tend to give way first. This may be your feet, your knees, or a particular muscle or tendon. No matter where a chronic pain shows up, it is important to consider whether the reason may be overtraining. If you have been increasing your mileage, have added an extra workout, started at your old level after a layoff, or started running hills or intervals or speed work, then it is reasonable to suspect the increased load to be the source of your trouble. Go back to your old work load until the problem clears. Then raise your mileage (or speed or other stress) far more slowly and see whether you encounter the same trouble. It doesn't matter whether someone else has managed to increase at twice the rate you are trying, or even if you have done so in the past. You have to accept the verdict of your body as to how much stress it will tolerate today. Learn to do so gracefully and you will have few injuries.

Injuries caused by overstress may be difficult to distinguish from structural problems, particularly when you are increasing your work load. A knee problem that appears when you get up to fifty miles of training a week may be the result of too fast an increase or it may be due to a mild deformity that begins to bother you at this level of training. Rule out overstress first by reducing your mileage until the pain disappears and then increasing it just a little at a time. If the injury reappears, the problem may be struc-

The primary cause of injury among runners is overstress. The best runners are likely candidates, because they are able to push closer to their limits. Stressing your body will make it grow stronger, but if you push too far, it will break down.

tural. Overwork is the simplest problem to solve and an obvious thing to suspect when you have started to work harder. With all injuries, begin by looking for the most obvious answers and avoid the attraction of exotic explanations until all the common ones have failed. If you go back to a lower level of training and your pain disappears but then reappears at the same level of training no matter how slowly you build up to it, you have made an important diagnostic finding. You apparently either need a different balance of training or have a structural abnormality that has to be corrected to withstand the new level of stress.

Imbalanced Training

A lot of injuries that you might think result from overstress are best thought of as the result of ill-conceived training instead. The most important of these are the ones that could be prevented by proper stretching of the muscles and tendons. Hamstring pulls, calf-muscle pulls, Achilles-tendon problems (at least in their initial stages), and a lot of back problems fall into this category. Sprinters and hurdlers need to pay particular attention to stretching. Still other difficulties can be avoided before they start with strengthening of muscles that do not get enough exercise in running, particularly the abdominals and the muscles of the front of the leg (see chapter 8).

Similarly, excessive speed work, intervals, or hill training without adequate endurance preparation is likely to cause injuries, and these are caused as much by improper division of the work as by sheer quantity. When sudden shifts of training are made, you have to watch for signs of overuse. Moving from fifty miles per week on the flats to the same distance on hills or doing hard intervals may or may not be tolerated. At the first signs of overtraining, ease up for a few days.

Structural Problems

Although structural problems in the runner's body are not responsible for nearly as many injuries as the two causes just described, they are at the root of the most frustrating and refractory ailments. They can be difficult to diagnose, particularly if the runner does not have access to one of the rare specialists with a good understanding of this field of medicine, primarily podiatrists (foot specialists) with an interest in sports medicine.

Whereas the upper body plays a more important role in running than most people realize and the legs provide the motive power, it is the feet that underlie everything else. They are complex parts of the body and are usually forgotten—until they start to hurt or to transmit ailments up the legs. Hurting feet cannot be ignored; they have a way of attracting attention in a very effective manner. Furthermore, the way the foot contacts the ground provides both the shock absorption for the rest of the body during running and the foundation for its movement. A defect in the way that the foot lands on the ground results in sideways force being exerted on the ankle. If the ankle is weak, then trouble results there. If it is strong, the force is transmitted to the knee, which either yields to the imbalanced force or passes it on to the hips. At some critical level of stress, the weakest joint, tendon, ligament, or muscle begins to show signs of the heavy load and starts to give way. Several may begin to give way at once.

Alternately, the runner may unconsciously compensate for a distorted foot by placing extra stress somewhere else. Again, the eventual result is likely to be a chronic injury at the weakest part of the lower body. The cause is the way the foot contacts the ground, but this is often concealed in subtle ways and can be very hard to diagnose. Besides, by the time correct diagnosis takes place, complications may have developed that are far worse than the original problem.

A summary of some of the most common foot-related problems follows. It is not complete, both because a thorough listing is far beyond the scope of this book and because a listing of exotic problems is likely to distract the runner's attention from the far more likely explanations mentioned here. The discussion later in this chapter of specific maladies mentions some of the structural imperfections that may cause them.

Although various structural abnormalities are common in the population, these often cause no difficulty unless the body is stressed beyond a certain level. This is why runners are more likely to encounter such injuries than is the average person.

Abnormalities of the Legs and Feet

Podiatrists have a unique definition of the word *normal*, because under their definition the majority of the population has feet that are abnormal. Nevertheless, the definition works well in treating a host of runners' ailments. A normal foot may be defined functionally as one that does not place twisting stresses on the ankles, knees, or hips and is not unusually stressed itself—that is, a foot that does not twist and torque the rest of the leg when you stand or walk normally, but simply falls straight and flat on the floor in line with the leg. To perform this function the calcaneus, or heel bone, has to be vertical and the forefoot must naturally come into contact with the ground in a flat position. (The outside of the foot normally contacts the ground first, but at mid-stride the heel should be straight and the whole forefoot on the ground.) The legs have to be very close to the same length, and the arch needs to follow a roughly normal configuration. The foot has to be able to rotate down onto the ground smoothly to reach the neutral position and has to be able to function as a rigid lever during the forward thrust of a stride as the body is pushed off the forefoot. The legs have to fall in a fairly straight line from the hips to the feet to transfer the weight of the body normally.

Unequal leg length. Most people have some difference in the length of their legs. Unless the difference is great, it usually goes unnoticed, but even very small differences sometimes cause problems, particularly for runners. The foot may be pinched up at the arch and the heel cords tightened to compensate, and the pelvis may tip, which also causes the spine to curve in the opposite direction. A whole series of complaints can result from these compensating shifts of the body. They include foot problems from the pinched-up arch, low-back pain, and pains caused by nerve injury, particularly shooting pains down the back of the thigh and leg. A moderate difference in the length of the legs can be easily treated either by shoe inserts or modification of one heel wedge, but it may be quite difficult to detect, even for a podiatrist or orthopedist skilled in making leg measurements.

Other leg abnormalities. Bowlegs, knock-knees, a pigeon-toed gait, or one in which the feet point outward all indicate deformities in the joints of the hips or the legs. The imbalances created are naturally transferred down to the feet, which may have to twist into odd positions to try to compensate. This compensation in turn can create additional stresses. Anyone with a fairly obvious condition of this type will probably be aware of it. If overuse injuries begin to occur, it is reasonable to assume that stresses due to the leg abnormalities may be at fault. Minor compensations may be attempted on one's own, but it seems sensible to see a sports-oriented podiatrist if you have any of these problems, since compensation that is likely to produce the best compromises for both performance and comfort is quite complex when significant abnormality of the legs is present.

Angulation of the heel and forefoot. The foot has a neutral position, the one it assumes when the weight of the body is being transmitted directly down through the leg and the foot is flat on the ground. Ideally, when the foot is in this neutral position, the heel bone should be squarely below the ankle bone. The heads of the metatarsals, the five long bones that extend through the foot to the base of the toes, should all rest on the ground. The foot is normally in this neutral position in the middle of each stride, as the body passes over it. Most people have some variations from the normal attitude when the foot is in the neutral position, however. The joint above the heel bone may be irregular so that the heel tilts to either the outside or the inside when the foot is in the neutral position. If the bottom of the heel tilts out, the condition is called valgus heel; if it tilts in, it is a varus heel.

Even if the heel and ankle are in a perfectly vertical line, the forefoot may not drop flat onto the ground. The metatarsal heads on the inside—those associated with the big toe and the next one or two—may not all drop to the ground when the heel is neutral. To bring the whole forefoot in contact with the ground the foot then has to tilt inward, or pronate. This condition, known as forefoot varus, is one of the more common abnormalities. (The foot pronates during normal walking and running, but this and other abnormalities cause it to do so before it should and more than it should.)

If, when the heel is in the neutral position, the outside metatarsal heads—those associated with the little toe and the next one or two—don't rest on the ground, the foot will tend to roll to the outside. The condition is known as forefoot valgus. People may have varying degrees and combinations of varus or valgus in the heel and forefoot. The more variation there is from the vertical, the more likely the runner is to have trouble.

Flatfeet. Feet are hardly ever really flat. If you have what are usually called flatfeet, you can probably see a perfectly normal arch when you raise your foot to look at it. If the foot rolls in (pronates) when placed on the ground and weighted, the arch disappears because it has rolled over on its side. Typically, this will be the result of a fair amount of varus in the forefoot, but there may be other causes.

High arch. A very high arch (cavus foot) tends to be rather inflexible and to provide inadequate shock absorption. It can result in a good many overstress injuries, and serious nerve injuries may result from it. Since the problem tends to progress to more severe stages and to bring about a number of nasty chronic injuries, anyone who has it and has any difficulties at all should see a good podiatrist.

Morton's foot. A foot with a short, floppy first metatarsal, which may show easily when the big toe is shorter than the second toe, is called Morton's foot. The foot tends to roll in the way it does with a forefoot varus. The second metatarsal is prone to stress fractures, because it takes most of the force that would normally be put on the first one.

Common Injuries

Shin splints. The classic overuse injury of the beginner and of the runner just starting to train again after a long layoff is shin splints, pains, sometimes merely annoying and sometimes quite severe, along either side of the front of the lower bone of the leg. Generally, the pain concentrates around the shins just above the ankle, but it may extend almost up to the knee. A variety of actual structures may be involved. There may be inflammation of the tendons running down to the foot from the muscles along the front of the leg, mild injury of the muscles themselves, or some tearing of the connecting tissue between the muscle and the bone.

In diagnosing the cause of shin splints, it is important to examine your training carefully. If you have just started training, come back after a layoff, increased your normal load, or switched to a different type of training (hills, soft surfaces to hard pavement, etc.), the reason for the shin splints is obvious. Work into the new routine a little more easily and take some time to exercise and stretch the muscles on the front of the lower leg. Do the stretching before and after the run. Shin splints may also result after bruising or blistering of the toes or the front of the foot, because the shin muscles are used to hold back the forefoot to keep it from hitting hard. Ice packs or soaking in cold water can provide symptomatic relief and minimize the problem.

Chronic shin-splint problems can be caused by a foot abnormality that needs correction by shoes that are either too stiff at the ball of the foot or too loose, allowing the foot to slip around.

Achilles tendonitis. One of the most common of runners' injuries is Achilles tendonitis. If it is allowed to progress and worsen, it can become chronic and very difficult to manage, because the sheath of the tendon may thicken to protect it, consequently causing permanent constriction unless corrective surgery is done. Alternatively, the excessive stress may cause the tendon to be partially or completely ruptured. All the muscles of the calf tend to be shortened in most people from lack of stretching, and runners greatly worsen the tendency by strengthening and shortening those muscles further. The primary preventive and corrective measure for Achilles tendonitis is stretching. This is an easy area of the body to stretch. It can be done almost anywhere, at odd moments during the day. Besides the stretch shown in the preceding chapter, it is easy to devise others.

When you are actually suffering from tendonitis, stretching extensively before and after running is critical. Avoid training that stresses the Achilles excessively, such as hill and speed work. Make sure that your shoes provide good cushioning and have a good heel lift, and take it easy until the condition improves. Don't try to increase mileage; cut it down instead. If the pain increases, particularly during running, lay off until it is better. Ice packs or cold water will help.

Foot deformities can help to precipitate Achilles tendonitis, though stretching will usually prevent it from developing. If, however, you can't control it fairly quickly, see a podiatrist. Trying to run through pain with tendonitis getting a little worse every day is crazy; it almost guarantees developing a long-term problem.

Knee problems. Problems of the knee may result from structural imbalances; from overstress, particularly if you have old knee injuries; or from a combination of the two. Running down hills commonly causes knee pain, especially if you aren't used to it. As always, look for obvious causes first: overtraining, new shoes, changes in training patterns, and so forth. Excessive shoe wear is another common cause; if one side of the sole, particularly the heel, is worn down more than an eighth-inch more than the other side, you may begin to feel pain in the knee.

Runner's knee (chondromalacia of the patella), one of the most common complaints, involves the wearing down of the cartilage behind the kneecap, often as a result of a structural imbalance. As for symptoms, a grinding sound in the knee is common; the knee is likely to be stiff in the morning or after you've been sitting for a long time; climbing and going down stairs is likely to be painful; and if you feel around the kneecap with your fingers, the bottom edge is likely to be sore. If you straighten your leg and lift it up to the horizontal and then push on the kneecap, it will be painful.

Although weak quadriceps muscles are not a cause of runner's knee, they do aggravate the problem. Quadriceps exercises may help to alleviate symptoms, because the stronger quads help to pull the kneecap into its proper position.

The most likely causes of knee injuries are overtraining, changes in training, shoe changes, and worn shoes. Running constantly on angled surfaces, such as a banked track or roads with pronounced crowns, can also cause knee problems. So can running around a small course in the same direction so that the force resulting from going around curves always stresses the legs the same way.

If these potential causes are eliminated and the pain persists, structural difficulties are probably the cause of your knee troubles, particularly if you found that they began at a certain training level. Excessive pronation of the feet, perhaps because of forefoot varus or Morton's foot, is a likely cause. Correction of these imbalances, either with home remedies such as arch cookies (for excessive pronation) or with orthotics fit by a podiatrist, usually brings relief within a few weeks. If your home remedies don't seem to be working within this time period, or the problem is worsening, seek a podiatrist.

Heel spurs and bumps. Very painful growths can develop on the bottom or back of the heel. They are caused initially by some form of persistent irritation that induces the foot to develop a fluid-filled sac under the skin near the bone. The sac becomes harder and fibrous as irritation continues and may finally develop into an actual growth on the bone in the area. The larger it grows, the more it tends to irritate the surrounding tendons, and when it becomes bony it may actually start to saw through them. A spur developing on the back of the heel irritates the Achilles tendon and may be caused by the rubbing against the heel of that tendon and the back of the shoe, often as the heel shifts because of an imbalance.

A bump on the bottom of the heel occurs where the band of muscles that are strung across the arch of the foot attach to the heel. This group of muscles is called the plantar fascia. Irritation of the plantar fascia at the attachment to the heel causes tenderness there, similar to a heel bump and resulting from similar causes.

A high arch can cause heel bumps, heel spurs, or irritation of the plantar fascia. So can excessive pronation of the foot. If you let these injuries go unattended, the bumps will get worse and eventually require surgical removal—and they will probably cause other problems along the way. Surgery is not a true solution, because the underlying cause still has to be treated. Therefore, unless your difficulties seem to have an obvious cause, such as a new or worn pair of shoes rather than a true structural problem, you should see a podiatrist who knows something about running injuries as soon as these difficulties start developing. (A stone bruise may cause similar symptoms, but the cause should be obvious, and the sensitivity should disappear rather quickly.) Intermediate relief can be had by using a piece of felt or foam with the center cut out as a cushion, or cutting out the back of the heel of the shoe to relieve a bump there. Be sure that your shoes have a good heel lift. You should either stop running or reduce the stress until the problem is corrected. Avoid hills and speed work until it is.

Stress fractures. Breaks in bones caused by excessive force from the normal act of running are known as stress fractures. They may occur in the lower bones of the leg and in the ankle, but runners most commonly experience stress fractures of the metatarsal bones. Usually, there is a crack in the bone rather than a complete break. Sometimes such breaks are hard to detect, and they always have to be positively diagnosed by X ray. If you have a severe pain or a persistent ache that suddenly starts and does not improve or that prevents you from running, see a podiatrist or orthopedist. Any runner can develop stress fractures, and some traumatic fractures caused by stepping in a hole or from a similar cause may result in the same symptoms without your having been aware of the break initially. People with Morton's foot and some other deformities are particularly prone to stress fractures. Fortunately, the bone grows back stronger than ever, so a runner can take some comfort in the thought that he will be less prone to the same injury. Correction for abnormalities with orthotics or other supports may help to avoid stress fractures to begin with.

Muscle pulls. A muscle pull may occur in any of the muscles involved with running, particularly if one tries to do strenuous work without a proper warm-up. Proper stretching as a regular routine eliminates almost all muscle pulls. Hamstrings and calves are the most likely muscles to pull. Typically, the runner initially feels a twinge, but often the muscle doesn't really start to hurt until later.

If you have structural defects, particularly in your feet, they will probably begin to cause difficulties at a particular level of conditioning. If the problem is left uncorrected, you risk chronic complications.

Chilling the muscle with an ice pack or cold water is some help. Keep your workouts easy until the pull has healed, with special emphasis on stretching and warm-up.

Chronic susceptibility to muscle pulls may be due to imbalanced development of the opposing muscles. Runners with weak quadriceps are subject to pulled hamstrings. So are bicyclists with very strong quads when they begin running. The solution is to strengthen the weak group of muscles.

Sprains. Sprains are traumatic injuries caused by a misstep, slip, or similar accident. Most frequently the runner will turn an ankle, and the result can range from a minor twinge to a major sprain or break. If you just have to hobble for a little way and then the ankle gets better, you probably don't need to worry, except for taking special care not to repeat the accident for a while. A slightly turned ankle tends to remain weak for some time and is vulnerable to more serious injury. Beware also of the anaesthetic effect that occurs soon after a more serious injury, which may last for a few hours. This is one of the protective tools of the body. It enables you to get home despite a possibly incapacitating injury, but it also may tempt you to keep running and risk an even more grave injury. Remember that it is generally impossible to tell a bad sprain from a break without X rays. If you are in doubt, see a doctor.

Runners frequently manage to turn a minor sprain into a major one or to delay healing by going out and running on the injury too soon. Don't! If you run on trails or other irregular terrain, be sure that your shoes are stable; some are much sloppier than others. Flexing and exercising the ankles in all directions is helpful in both preventing and recuperating from sprains. Chilling with ice or cold water reduces pain and swelling and may speed healing.

Back pains. Pains in the back may result from overtraining, inadequate stretching, fatigue, structural problems like unequal leg length, or weak abdominal muscles. Try stretching and doing abdominal exercises first. If you have chronic difficulties, you might see a podiatrist before heading for the orthopedic surgeon.

Nerve ailments. Chronic pains, bumps, and other problems may be caused by various nerve ailments. If they occur in the feet, see a podiatrist unless they go away soon. These sorts of pains should not be allowed to continue if they are at all severe or if they seem to be getting worse. Running can result in pinching, constricting, or damaging many different nerves. These ailments are rare, but they can be most unpleasant if you suffer from them.

One nerve problem that is easy to recognize is sciatica, a stabbing or shooting pain that follows the course of the sciatic nerve from the lower back, through the buttocks, and down the inside back of the thigh, lower leg, and into the foot and big toe. It is caused by some irritation of the nerve and may be the result of lower-back problems or a difference in the length of the legs. The lower-back problems can be caused by weak abdominal muscles. See a doctor. You may want to see a podiatrist if you don't get prompt relief.

A Final Word on Injuries

Most runners' injuries are completely preventable. They are the result of predictable overstress. Your body can only take so much. Watch for warning signs, and heed them. Do your warm-ups, stretches, and supplementary exercises religiously. In the case of structural difficulties and other chronic problems, you will almost always have plenty of warning before things get serious. Minor discomforts and pains are inevitable sometimes in running, but when the pain begins to exceed this level, the time has come to stop ignoring it. It is a friendly warning, and things will get worse if you don't heed the signals. If you can't figure out what is wrong and the solutions you try don't work, seek medical help. Don't be passive: if the doctor tells you in an offhand way to take two aspirins and stop running, go elsewhere. A podiatrist who is interested in runners is usually the best bet.

What the podiatrist can often do in the case of structural problems is to construct a support that changes the surface your foot meets to one offering proper support. A forefoot varus requires a raised surface under the inside ball of the foot so that the inside metatarsals receive support when the heel is in the neutral phase. A heel tilted the wrong way needs an angled support and perhaps a post that prevents it from tipping over too far. Typically, after initial examination, and perhaps correction of complications that have developed, the podiatrist will strap the foot and tape on some experimental padding to provide limited correction. Unequal leg length might be corrected with a lift in one shoe. If the experimental strapping and padding seem to help, a soft orthotic may be molded out of special foam that conforms to the shape of the foot in the neutral position. When placed in the running or street shoe, the orthotic partially supports the foot against rolling into abnormal positions. Some people find that soft orthotics give sufficient support. Others require later fitting of a rigid or semirigid orthotic, usually made from acrylic plastic. Such orthotics, when properly fitted, can enable most people to run pain-free.

It is important to demand that the orthotics work. They are expensive, and the job of fitting them and choosing the proper compromises in correction is subtle and difficult. You have to make the effort to get used to orthotics, but if you do, they ought to do the job. The podiatrist should be able and willing to adjust them until they do.

Heat-induced Illness

The dangers of overheating during distance running have already been mentioned in a number of contexts. A combination of high temperatures, high humidity, and direct sunlight can place tremendous additional stress on the distance runner, who generates a great deal of excess heat that the body must get rid of. Heat poses particular dangers to athletes who have not acclimatized recently and whose bodies are thus not prepared to deal with the problem.

Cramps are common during and after hot-weather races or long runs and are probably caused mainly by a loss of both fluid and electrolytes from the muscles. Drink electrolyte-replacement beverages, stretch, and try to keep walking or jogging for some time after the run.

Heat exhaustion occurs frequently and is the most common form of serious heat-induced illness during races and long runs in hot weather. Watch for it in yourself and in those around you. During heat exhaustion, the body loses control of circulation in the capillaries at the skin. These expand too much to aid cooling, and the blood pools in them so that there is not enough blood pressure to maintain adequate supplies to the brain. The victim is likely to feel nauseated, dizzy, and weak. The skin may be pale and clammy. Body temperature remains approximately normal, perhaps a little cool. The pupils of the eyes may be dilated, and some confusion and incoherence is common.

The victim of heat exhaustion needs to lie down in the shade with the feet elevated so that enough blood gets to the brain. He should be provided with moderate quantities of electrolyte-replacement fluids, but not be forced to drink. He is quite likely to faint and possibly be injured in the process if he stands up. He should be watched in case heat stroke begins to develop.

Heat stroke is a major emergency, since it can quickly cause brain damage and death. It is caused by a breakdown of the body's normal cooling system, including the cessation of perspiration. The skin is red, dry, and very hot. Body temperature skyrockets. Pulse is strong. The victim must be rapidly cooled by any means available: fanning, application of ice, immersion in water, or any other expedient. Cooling must be continued until body temperature approaches normal, and medical attention should be obtained as quickly as possible. A person who has already been cooled needs to be watched in case the syndrome begins again.

Shoe Modifications

Many runners with structural problems in their feet have found that inserts or minor shoe modifications are sufficient to allow them to run trouble-free. It is important to exercise great care if you decide to experiment, in order to avoid chronic injuries, and many may choose to visit a podiatrist instead if they suspect structural problems.

One easy problem to solve is the inability to find shoes to fit a narrow heel. Adhesive foam with a soft nap surface can be purchased at medical supply houses and cut to fit both sides of the heel inside the shoe. Nylon-backed neoprene foam can be glued in with contact cement to form a more permanent support. Bevel the edges of either material with scissors to make them smooth.

Excessive motion of the forefoot in one direction or the other may be controllable by adding foam or similar materials inside the shoe or may require rigid orthotics cast by a podiatrist. If it is clear, for example, that your foot is pronating excessively, try putting adhesive foam along the ball and arch area, taping it in place, and running for a few days. If your condition improves, glue identical patches of surgical felt or nylon-backed neoprene foam, obtainable in diving and kayaking shops, inside your shoes, and see if they help. I have found that firm rubber "arch cookies," which can be bought in three sizes from running shops or directly from New Balance Shoe Company, 38-42 Everett St., Boston, MA 02134, solve the problems caused by my excessive pronation. After trying the cookies' positions carefully, I glue smooth nylon fabric on the tops and glue them into my shoes with contact cement. Others have found Dr. Scholl's supports helpful.

Adhesive-backed, nap-faced foam is also useful for cutting doughnut-shaped pads to relieve pressure on blisters, corns, bunions, and heel spurs.

10 / *Competition*

Some runners are naturally competitive about running and gravitate to racing at an early stage. For many others, racing is the antithesis of everything attractive about running. One can, after all, enjoy a lifetime of running without ever competing in a race. Probably the majority of experienced runners regard racing as another aspect of the sport, one that demonstrates the level of excellence that can be achieved by the talented and hard-working and that provides useful goals for the average runner who wants to achieve personal improvement.

Races provide social occasions in what is generally a fairly antisocial sport. Even at higher levels of competition, most runners are friendly and open when they get together at races, enjoying one another's company and taking genuine pleasure at others' performances. You may run step for step against someone of your own talent and ability in a race, while the leaders are far ahead. The immediate rivalry is a spur to do your best, but your real competition is with the course and with yourself. There are a lot of contradictions and variations in such attitudes, of course, but at races there is generally much camaraderie among runners at all levels of competition.

Distance running is unique among competitive sports in its democratic nature. Most races are open to all comers, with only slight concessions, if any, made to star performers. In what other sport can the middle-aged duffer compete with international champions? Moreover, the less-talented or older runner can achieve victories as well as personal satisfaction. The elation of the novice competing in a first ten-mile race or marathon or of the intermediate runner finally achieving a personal time goal in such a race is every bit as great as the winner's satisfaction. Age-group competition and handicap races, in which the odds are adjusted so that runners beginning from different levels can compete on equal footing, are held frequently.

Whether or not racing appeals to you in itself, you are a beneficiary of the training methods developed by racers and their coaches, as they have tested most of the techniques that improve performance. The crucible of competition clearly separates routines that work from those that do not. Racing also provides a common beginner's goal that helps to provide a focus for training and the impetus to get out of bed on cold winter mornings. The objective may be simply to finish a particular race. Running a marathon is a theme common to many runners, and once this is accomplished, the runner may decide to try to complete another in a specific time.

After you have been running for a while, it is difficult not to take an interest in the accomplishments of some of the best racers. There is a sense of marvel at the level of performance achieved by really good runners. You may also feel the satisfaction of partici-

Weekend road races such as this one are becoming commonplace in every part of the United States. They provide an opportunity for runners to measure themselves against others and a social occasion in a generally antisocial sport.

pating in your own way in the exploration of the limits of the body, which is one of the goals of racing and of running in general.

I recall one dark winter morning as my running companion and I were finishing a long hill climb near my home with our usual sprint up the last quarter of a mile. As we passed our understood finish line and trotted on up a final slope, panting for breath, I asked him, in between gasps, if it had ever occurred to him that Frank Shorter runs an entire marathon faster than we could sprint that short distance. The fact that we can never hope to approach the level of performance of a Shorter does not, however, diminish our enjoyment of our own personal victories.

Attitudes toward Competition

In thinking about races and training for them (if that is what you want to do), it is important to have an accurate idea about your own attitudes. People who run mainly for fun or general fitness and who have no strong competitive instincts don't need to think a lot about racing. They really need only pay enough attention to be sure that they are in satisfactory condition for any races that they do run and that they work out the logistics well enough to ensure that they will enjoy the experience.

Natural racers need to be somewhat more careful. Racing is important to them, so they will be unhappy if they do less than their best because of inadequate planning. Moreover, their drive is likely to lead them to injuries and poor performances if it is not guided by strategy both in training and racing. This is especially true of a lot of gifted runners, who can manage fast times through sheer talent but who are liable to break down if they don't develop the endurance to go with their speed.

Strong competitors are likely to start racing with minimal training. In fact, their training runs often become races, either against companions or against the clock. This attitude quickly becomes self-defeating. Dramatic progress cannot continue indefinitely, and even if injury does not occur, the highly competitive runner is likely to become disappointed after hitting the inevitable plateau and watching performance level off or decline.

Long-term goals may therefore be even more important for the competitive runner than for the casual one. You must decide

what races you are training for, set up appropriate training schedules, and avoid burning yourself out in a year or two. This is as
much the case for the young runner as for the middle-aged one,
and coaching programs for young runners should emphasize enjoyment of running and personal development over the years,
rather than immediate competitive goals. The practice of having
high-school track teams compete two or three times a week is fool-
ish. Similarly, mature runners who compete too often in too many
long races are asking for trouble. Such racing may do no harm if
the races are run like training runs, at less than full effort, but if
they are run all-out, they will eventually break the runner down.

It is important to realize that for the distance runner, racing at
a level of maximum performance is different from training. Training builds up the body's reserves by stressing the body at a level
that stimulates it to become stronger. Racing taps the reserves,
both physical and psychological, that have been built up. All-out
racing is always a strain on the body, and too much racing will
break the system down. The amount of racing that the body will
tolerate varies a good deal from one individual to another. For anyone, however, the results of too many hard races too close together
are likely to be disastrous. As with overtraining, the body gives
warning signs, but these can be ignored by a fit individual—for a
while.

As a general rule, it is rarely a good idea to run another race
until you have run ten times the distance of the last one in training
mileage. Thus, if you normally run fifty miles a week, you should
wait a week before repeating a five-mile race. This lapse is a minimum, which is insufficient for regular repetition. Your overall proportion of racing miles should be far lower than 10 percent. Somewhere between 2 and 5 percent of overall training mileage is the
range in which most people can race safely. Of course, we are talking about all-out racing here. You can go out and race every week
for fun, provided you keep the races in which you put out maximum effort within the proper limits.

These figures are meant as rough estimates. Much depends on
your own body's resilience and on the type of racing you do. Short
races are generally less of a strain on the body than long ones. Marathons and longer distances in particular produce a degree of stress
out of proportion to their distance. Most runners have to draw

heavily on their deep reserves in order to run races of this length at their personal capacities. Most racers find that a marathon takes far more out of them than a twenty-mile race, and a two-mile or five-mile race is far less stressful than a ten-miler. Conditions must also be taken into account. A marathon in hot, muggy weather will be much harder on your body, even if you are heat acclimatized, than one run in pleasant, cool conditions.

Finding the Races

The number of races held regularly varies a lot from one region of the country to another. Overall, there are vastly more than there were a few years ago, and the quantity and variety are growing steadily. In some parts of the nation, particularly New England and California, there are likely to be a variety of races on any weekend within an hour or two's drive. The selection may be a little sparser elsewhere, but perseverance will turn up quite a few.

Many local running clubs sponsor races on a regular basis, often at a number of levels of organization. The most loosely put together are the "fun runs," which may be set up as races or simply as collective training runs, depending on the location and the inclination of the participants. In any case, the general atmosphere is informal, no sanction is sought from official governing bodies, and times are usually called out to the runners as they finish, with the runners recording their own, if any recording is done at all. Usually there is no entry fee and no awards are given unless the run follows some unique course, in which case souvenir prizes may be given, usually to all finishers.

More formal races may include handicap races or age-group and sex divisions, both discussed below. Such classifications are designed to provide some of the fun of competition to everyone, either by equalizing the odds among all the runners or by breaking them down into groups with comparable physical endowment. In age-group competition, for example, fifty-year-old men run with everyone else but compete only against one another.

Many races are sanctioned by nationwide governing groups such as the AAU, the United States Track and Field Federation, or the Road Runners Club of America. Such groups certify that courses are properly measured. Times may qualify participants for

various limited-entry races, such as national or regional championships. They also ensure certain uniformity of rules. There is a good
deal of controversy among runners and local clubs concerning the
policies of the AAU, which is the primary governing organization
for amateur running competition in the United States. At some
races, the runner may be asked to join the AAU in order to compete, and part of the fees collected from competitors in any sanctioned race goes to the organization. The arguments are too involved to be aired here, and they are not likely to be of much
concern to the runner just beginning to enter races.

Many races are listed in advance in various runners' publications, particularly *Runner's World* and *Track and Field News*. In
particular areas of the country, local publications and club newslet-
ters are likely to be the best sources of information. Talk to the
runners you meet on the roads or tracks to find out about local or-
ganizations. Once you find a local race, the people there should be
able to tell you everything else you need to know.

Because of the great boom in distance running, runners interested primarily in shorter distances or in events like the hurdles or
steeplechase may have a harder time finding races than road runners. This is particularly true for age-group racing. Short distances
are not as amenable to casual timing methods as road races, either.
If no short-distance events are held in your area, the best solution
may be to find a few other interested runners and try to start a program under the umbrella of a local club. Nearly all races are organized completely by runners who want them anyhow, so pursue
your own goals. A lot of the necessary equipment may be borrowed
from local schools, if you can find a sympathetic high school or
college coach.

Distance-race Organization

The quality of race organization varies tremendously from one
competition to another, as do the requirements the people putting
the race on must deal with. The primary problem for the orga-
nizers of a race like the Boston Marathon is the handling of the volume of entrants and spectators. At Boston they don't have to worry
about getting enough publicity, but rather about keeping reporters
from getting in the way of the race while still allowing them to see

it. For most races, publicity is hard to obtain, assuming the orga-
nizers want it, and their attention concentrates on proper course
measurement, timing of the contestants, getting word of the race
to the runners who may be interested, providing beverage stations
for long races, and traffic control and relations with the police and
public.

The single most important organizational task for races that are
not run on a track is accurate measurement of the course. Automobile odometers are notoriously inaccurate, and even if they
have been calibrated, they are only accurate enough to plot out a
rough distance prior to exact measurement. Several methods can
be used for final measurement. Short distances can be measured
off with a steel tape and then permanently marked with spray paint
or by spikes driven into the asphalt. (It is a good idea to put in a
permanent mark off the pavement at each side of the road, so that
any later resurfacing of the road does not require that the whole
operation be redone.)

For longer courses, the exact method required is usually specified by any governing organization approached for sanction, so it is
well to check with them in advance if you want certification.
Usually either a surveyor's wheel or a bicycle with a rotation
counter mounted on the front wheel is used. A standard distance,
usually a mile, is measured out on a straight stretch of road with a
steel tape and permanently marked. Then before measurement of
any course, the surveyors' wheel or bicycle is calibrated over the
standard distance. Remember that tire wear and similar factors can
change the number of revolutions per mile significantly, so recali-
bration is important before measurement of any new course. Blow
up tires to a high pressure before calibration, and be sure that if a
bicycle is used, the same rider pedals over both the calibration
rides and the course (the weight of the rider can affect the measurement). In measuring a road course, the route actually to be followed by the runners should be taken, cutting the insides of
corners where appropriate and using the shortest course.

On long courses each mile or kilometer should be marked.
More frequent intervals should be designated on shorter courses.
During races it is desirable to have timers at specified intervals to
call out "splits" to the racers—that is, to give them their times so
that they can check their pace. Where logistics permit, it is also

customary for these callers to inform each racer of his or her place in the field. Checkpoints are placed where they are needed to record the numbers of the passing runners to prevent anyone from shortcutting the course or to ensure that the number of laps each runner has completed is kept track of.

Any race over ten miles should have aid stations every few miles where runners can get drinks. Many top racers prefer to have their own mixtures at such stations. Customarily, at most races, the competitor is offered a choice of water or an electrolyte replacement drink in a paper cup, which he can toss away on the run. There must be enough fluid for all the people running and enough personnel at each station to fill cups fast enough during the time when the greatest rush occurs. Provisions also have to be made to clean up afterward. The electrolyte replacement drinks should be of the commercial variety (ERG, Body Punch, Gatorade, or whatever), and the type should be called out to the runners as they approach, since many people cannot tolerate some brands. The largest turnout that might possibly occur and the hottest weather should be anticipated in planning drinks. It is worse to promise aid stations and inadequately stock them than not to have them at all. At least if a runner knows there will be no drinks, he or she can plan on supplying personal needs.

Sanctioned races have elaborate timing requirements. For a less strictly organized race, any standard timing device will do. Digital timers that have a function for reading out individual times while the main clock continues to run are now relatively inexpensive and convenient.

Advance registration is commonly required to allow officials to plan on drinks, awards, and the like. The fee that is charged covers race expenses, including promotion. Promoters of large races often pay expense money to famous runners to ensure a high level of competition and to attract other racers. The costs of advertising and mailing out information and entry forms are not negligible.

Some of these details are mentioned to give the beginner an idea of the work that goes into running a successful race. But let the racer beware: not all races are well organized. Inadequately stocked and staffed aid stations are common, for example. Run your races for fun, and be prepared to take any little hardships along the way in stride. If you should ever help organize a race, do your best to be sure that you don't make the same mistakes. Try to remember to thank the people who put the race together. They are nearly always volunteers and rarely recover all their expenses.

Distances

Races are run over a wide variety of distances, some of them officially recognized and others dictated by convenience or the length of some naturally attractive course. Separate records are generally recognized for indoor and outdoor track times, with road and cross-country races considered a separate category. World competitions are now all held over metric distances, which are gradually becoming more common in the United States. Thus, the 100-meter dash has replaced the 100-yard distance in international competition, and the 800-meter race is run instead of the 880-yard,

The form of a master. Frank Shorter, one of the great long-distance racers of all time, is the far runner at the finish of a local fun run.

or half-mile. The most common distance events are the steeple-chase (a 3,000-meter artificial cross-country course with 28 hurdles and seven water jumps); 2 miles; 3 miles; 5,000 meters; 5 miles; 6 miles; 10,000 meters; 10 miles; 20,000 meters; 15 miles; 25,000 meters; 30,000 meters; 20 miles; 25 miles; the marathon (26 miles, 385 yards); 30 miles; 50,000 meters; 40 miles; 50 miles; 100 miles; and 24 hours. Cross-country races are also distance races with both distance and terrain varying somewhat. (To convert between metric and U.S. measurements, remember that 1,000 meters, or 1 kilometer, equals ⅝ of a mile. A mile, naturally, is ⁸/₅ of a kilometer.)

In the United States the traditional track seasons have been an outdoor track season in the spring, a cross-country season in the fall, and an indoor track season in winter. Road races do not really follow this seasonal pattern, however, and most runners are more likely to compete in road races. Typically, the road-racing season follows the local climatic pattern, with few serious races in winter except in the southern states, on the West Coast, and in Hawaii. In most states the bulk of road racing occurs in spring and summer, with fun runs often filling in the rest of the year.

For the beginner who wants to start racing, probably the best strategy, just as with training, is to start out with longer distances at moderate speeds. Distances like the mile, run at maximum effort, are best left until you have a good conditioning base. If you are running two or three miles a day regularly, you should be able to handle a five-mile road race. If you are running four or five miles a day, you could manage up to a ten-mile race at the beginning. Try to do a couple of races in this range and gain some experience with pacing before you go out for longer, more taxing races.

Tactics

Tactics are an important part of racing. Racers with good tactics have often been able to beat slightly faster runners, because they had better strategy. Tactics for beginners are different from those for experienced racers, however. After you have a number of races under your belt you will be better able to judge your own reserves, to plan and execute your pace, and so on. Novices who are still undergoing basic conditioning have to be particularly careful not to try to race hard and often. Even if you have a few successes, results will soon start to decline rather than improve if you race hard on inadequate reserves.

If, during your first couple of races, you are racing distances that are twice as far as your daily average, don't try to run the first three-quarters of the race any faster than your normal training pace. Once you are this far along, if you still feel that you have plenty of reserve energy, speed up your pace gradually and sprint at the finish. The normal mistake that everyone makes at the start, however, is to go out too fast. One is automatically caught up in the euphoria of the race. The fast pace feels easy—for a while. Neophytes are also less sure of their own pace and have a hard time judging how fast they are going. Somewhere between the half and three-quarter marks, reality suddenly intrudes and you hit the wall. Your pace suddenly slows, every step requires an act of will-power, and you breathe harder at half your former speed than you did when you were really moving along. If this happens, don't feel discouraged. Everyone has done the same thing at least once. Learn your lesson, and pace yourself more efficiently the next time.

If you have run the distance of your first race a number of times before at your normal training pace, then you can race some-what faster. The same strictures about keeping your speed down apply, however. Try to set a realistic goal, perhaps running thirty seconds per mile faster than your training pace. Thus, if you're going to run a ten-mile race and you have run ten miles in eighty minutes without straining too much, you might reasonably try to run a ten-mile race in seventy-five minutes. During the week be-fore the race, try to run one mile during each training session at exactly this pace, or seven and a half minutes per mile. Concentrate on the way this pace feels. Then when you start your race, think only about that pace. Don't worry how fast anyone else is going; just accelerate to your own speed and hold it.

The most efficient race during normal conditions is always an evenly paced race. That is, you can run the fastest overall time of which you are capable if you run the whole race at one optimum speed. This omits certain strategic and psychological factors, but the beginner should leave them out anyway. You aren't going to be leading the Boston Marathon for quite a while, so you don't have to worry about how to break Bill Rodgers or Kim Merritt. Learning to pace yourself is one of the most valuable racing tactics you will ever learn. You will probably have a hard time doing it at first. You'll find yourself slowing as you go along, particularly if you don't concentrate on maintaining your pace.

Concentration is one of the most important tools of the serious racer. You may not want to worry about it, particularly during those races that you're running for training. It is often a lot more pleasant to chat with your fellow runners and just have a good time. On the other hand, if you really want to run the best race you can on a given day, it is vital to concentrate on your own pace. Without it, you will drift off mentally and either run too fast early in the race or slow down when you don't need to. Successful distance racers have to concentrate on what they are doing in a race just as much as a ski jumper or target shooter. They must monitor what is going on in their own bodies and on the course around them.

After you have run a few races, you will have a better idea of what your true capabilities are. If you finish in the time that you planned and feel bright and fresh, it is obvious that you can run a faster race if you want to. On the other hand, if you were forced to slow down a long way from the finish line, you need to start out slower next time. You'll also start to meet other racers who are close to your own level, and in future races you can mentally race against them, using this closer level of competition to bring out the best performances in yourself.

You have to learn to adjust your pacing to the conditions. If the weather is hot, you will not be able to run as fast a race. In fact, unless you have acclimatized yourself to the heat (as described in the next chapter), it will be dangerous to try to run fast at all. Slow way down, and drink as much as you possibly can. If it is very hot or you begin to feel woozy, cold, weak, or dizzy, *stop!* Remind yourself of the symptoms of heat injury discussed in the last chapter. Other conditions should also persuade you to slow your pace. If you are running into a twenty-five-mile-an-hour headwind, you just won't be able to go as fast. If you try, you'll break down long before the finish.

Make adjustments to your own conditions as well. Unless you are really ill, in which case you should not run at all, stick to your pace at least for the first mile, but if you are straining to maintain it after that, slow down. You may be running faster than you think you are, or you may be having a bad day. Nearly everyone has physical ups and downs, and if you try to push yourself at your best pace when you aren't feeling well, you'll be forced to slow down later on.

One exception you may want to make to the even-pace rule after your first few races results from the fact that there is much less wind resistance dragging on a runner if he or she "drafts" just behind someone else. This is especially true when there is a significant headwind, but even in still-air conditions a reasonably fast runner has to fight a lot of air drag. Thus, it may sometimes be worth running just a little faster than you otherwise would to stay with a group of competitors who are providing you with a wind shield. But this is true only when you have developed a good enough sense of pace to know that you're going only a little faster than planned. This also begins to open you up to the psychological traps that good competitors use to break the opposition. A racer will often periodically spurt off for some distance to demoralize the racers following. The person breaking away may be as taxed by the increased pace as those behind but has the advantage of knowing when the attack will come and how long it will last. The runners following are often broken by this sort of speed burst and drop off, exhausted psychologically as much as physically. The beginner will probably be physically broken indeed if he or she tries to keep up with such moves.

Infinite variations can be built out of combinations of the demoralizing effects on other racers when they think that they cannot maintain the pace set by the leader. Sometimes such tactics work, and sometimes they fail miserably. That is the stuff of which great races are made. For the newcomer, it is enough to keep two major points in mind. The first is that tactics become important only in deciding races between relatively evenly matched contestants. If you try to enter the game at a level that is much above you, you'll be wiped out long before the end of the race. Don't take the bait. Second, to repeat an earlier point, the most efficient race is an evenly paced one. Until you've determined the maximum pace at which you can run a given distance, you are better off forgetting about other tactics. Stick to the basics.

In pacing a long race, it is a good idea to figure out the intervals at which you should pass various checkpoints and jot them down on the back of your hand or on a card. It is often hard to make such calculations in your head in the middle of a race. This is particularly important in races of odd length, like the marathon, and on courses where proper mileage markers are lacking.

Hills, Trails, and Such

There is no substitute for experience in dealing with cross-country terrain, rough footing, or hills. In road races, if you run a hilly course but haven't had much experience with the hills, the best strategy is to take it easy and accept a moderate delay, rather than risk burning yourself out. Pacing on hills is a function of judgment, which can be gained only by running a lot of hills, and strength, which is acquired by training on them. Technique is not really very complicated. Don't try to stride up hills; take short steps and speed up the tempo as much as you dare. Obviously, you are going to become short of breath racing up a hard hill. The art is learning to make it up as fast as you can without developing so much of an oxygen debt that you are slowed down too much by the top. In particular, you want to be able to take advantage of the downhill on the other side if there is one or to resume your normal pace on the flat.

Try to stay erect when you are climbing a hill. Keep your buttocks tucked in and your arm action moderate. Big arm swings are worthless for hill climbing unless you are sprinting. On the downhill, let your legs move as fast as you can, but try to let gravity do the work. Concentrate on abdominal breathing to try to avoid stitches (sharp pains in the side), which are a big problem in downhill running because of the tendency to tense up the abdomen to absorb road shock. Keep your arms low for balance. You don't need much arm swing for downhill speed. Just lean forward to go faster.

Cross-country racing on trails should be approached with care until you've done a lot of training on rough terrain. Footing is critical, and efficient trail running takes a lot of practice. It is very easy to sprain an ankle unless you have done enough running on irregular surfaces to strengthen the ankles and to learn proper foot placement.

Marathons and Longer Races

The special problems of racing distances longer than twenty miles deserve separate consideration. One reason is that the additional strain imposed by such races on the body is hard to appreciate until it has been experienced. Although there are exceptions, perhaps for most women, runners normally find that a marathon or a longer race is very much more taxing and painful than a twenty-miler. In previous chapters, the function of getting enough training miles during the buildup for such a race has been mentioned. The rule of thumb is that one should average one-third the distance of the race daily over a period of several months to avoid hitting the wall.

In races of marathon length and longer, dehydration and heat dissipation are the factors limiting the runner, particularly in hot weather. To run these races in hot weather, the runner must acclimatize to heat ahead of time to avoid collapse. With five miles to go under the hot Boston sun, Joe Fleming (500) and Joseph Doran (927) show the effects of the heat and the sub-seven-minute-mile pace through the Newton hills.

Pacing and adequate fluid intake are critical if one is to avoid problems during long races. All the comments earlier on pacing apply with a vengeance to the longer distances. The first-time marathoner usually goes out too fast and finishes at a crawl, if he or she finishes at all. Don't underestimate the difficulty of these long races. Be very conservative in planning your pacing: you are going to put a lot into a marathon, and it is depressing to crash halfway through because you have foolishly expected some kind of miracle to occur. If the best ten-miler you've ever run took seventy minutes, you are not going to be able to run a marathon at seven-minute miles. Start out with eight-minute miles, and if you feel like speeding it up at the twenty-mile mark, go right ahead. Plan your pace carefully before every marathon, preferably after a training run that didn't feel too good, so as to promote a healthy feeling of realism.

Don't rush into your first marathon. Give yourself a couple of years of running and a number of shorter races to work up to it. You'll stand a better chance of enjoying the experience and of finishing the way you want to—tired but not half-dead—if you avoid taking one on too soon. If you really get the bug and you have to run one (and finish it) before you're really ready, pace yourself a couple of minutes lower per mile than your ten-mile pace. Then you'll be able to finish intact, even if you feel as though you're crawling instead of running. You may not believe it, but you'll also finish faster.

Ultramarathons, distances longer than the marathon, are even more grueling. The fifty- and hundred-mile runs are virtually impossible to finish without undergoing a good deal of pain. Extensive training and experience is required to undertake these distances. Don't even think about them until you've run a few successful marathons.

Age-group Racing

Many of the better-organized races these days have categories and awards for various age groups and both sexes. The exact breakdown depends on the sponsorship, size, and so on, and it probably isn't too important. What is important is the recognition that the body's capacity for speed diminishes with age, so that a comparable performance by a forty-five-year-old runner is not as fast as that of one aged twenty.

Organized veteran championships are now held at both the regional and national level as part of this same movement, and a few international competitions have been held as well. Age-group competition for women lags a little behind, but this situation is improving rapidly. Admission requirements in some of the limited races, like the Boston Marathon, have also been adjusted to make allowances for age and sex.

Typically, age groups are broken down by five- or ten-year divisions from thirty-five or forty on up. In some races there are categories for children as well, to encourage younger runners. Age-group records are often listed in statistical summaries now, especially for the more popular distances.

If you are an older person running in open races and want to measure your performance against those of younger runners, you might want to look up the age-adjusted point system devised by Ken Young and printed in the *Runner's World* booklet "Age of the Runner."

Handicap Races

Handicap races are one of the most interesting ways to allow people of widely varying abilities to enjoy racing at a local level. The best program I know of is the one that has been run for a number of years by the Rocky Mountain Road Runners. In addition to conventional races, every month or so they hold a handicap race over a distance of between two and ten miles. A new runner entering the program runs in one of the races against one of the club's scratch runners, who is given no handicap advantage. The new runner is then assigned a handicap based on the period he or she comes in behind the scratch runner. The system is computerized so the results from races of various lengths can be compared, racers' records maintained easily, and handicaps assigned for each race.

On entering the next race the new runner is given a handicap from the computer printout. The slowest runners with the largest handicaps start first and the fastest ones last. The handicaps are designed so that everyone should be able to finish at approximately the same time. Therefore, anyone has a chance to win on a given day if he or she runs as hard as possible. Each race result is programed into the computer so that as a runner improves, his or her handicap is reduced. There is an averaging system built into the program, however, so that one poor performance does not raise one's handicap and guarantee success in the next race.

This method ensures equal opportunity, and so assures a lot of excitement in each race. It also provides the individual with a continuous record of progress over time, as an improving runner's handicap is reduced. Alternating conventional races with handicap races also provides a basis for comparison.

11/Training Methods and Theories

Among serious runners a mythology has developed around training techniques. This may be partly because the application of such techniques is more an art than a science. The methods that are normally used are simple enough and have all been around for quite a long time. What is difficult is putting together a training program that will work for a particular individual. Some coaches encourage the mystique that has grown up around this process, because they are not entirely sure what they are doing themselves.

The tendency among many racers and would-be racers is to copy the training schedules of some currently successful international star, as though a training schedule were a recipe: mix in so much distance, so many intervals, and such and such a hill routine and out comes a 2:10 marathoner or a 27:30 ten-thousand-meter runner. Actually, of course, a training schedule is no such thing. Training is a deliberate stressing of the body in certain ways in order to improve its performance. Training that is not geared to the person who is doing it probably will not have the desired effect. Following someone else's training program blindly is like wearing someone else's eyeglasses. The ingredients may be the same as those in glasses prescribed for you, but the effect is likely to be disastrous.

The vast difference between individuals is one of the reasons why it is so difficult to determine the exact effects of particular types of training. Champions have been trained according to all sorts of theories and formulas, but there is no conclusive evidence that one or another training doctrine is markedly better than another. Most of the best runners today train on a mixture of various

A good training schedule is worked out for the individual, not simply copied from the one used by some successful champion.

training elements. Before discussing detailed programs further, some of the specific techniques should be defined.

Interval Training

Interval training was for many years *the* formula for success. It is still used exclusively by many coaches. Some experiments have indicated that it is a particularly effective way to train, though these are quite inconclusive when you try to apply them to experienced runners. Furthermore, the umbrella term *interval training* covers so many kinds of running that it is difficult even to know what someone means by it, unless he includes an example of the order, speed, and effort involved.

Interval training consists of a series of short runs, usually done at a fairly high level of effort, alternating with rest periods during which the runner walks, jogs, or runs at a slower pace to recuperate. Although some training has been done with long, slow intervals at an aerobic pace, intervals are generally intended to develop

For years the dominant form of training was fast intervals run on a track, with short rest periods in between. The method is still used exclusively by some runners and is perhaps the best technique for building up speed prior to a racing season.

speed and to accustom the body to function in spite of an oxygen debt. Intervals enable the runner to run fast anaerobically and then permit sufficient recovery to allow repetition of the same routine. Although there are an infinite number of possible interval routines, intervals are typically run in sets: a group of fast runs with short recoveries in between, then a longer recuperation walk or jog, then another set is run. A typical interval workout for a serious racer might be written out this way:

2-mile warm-up jog; 2×110, 2×220, 2×440, 2×880; jog 220 after each interval; 1 mile, jog 880; 1 mile, jog 880; 2×880, 2×440, 2×220, 2×110; jog 220 after each interval; 2-mile cool-down jog.

The runner following this routine jogs 2 miles to the track or around it, runs 110 yards at a sprint, jogs 220 yards, runs 110, jogs 220, runs 220, jogs 220, runs 220, jogs 220, runs 440, jogs 220, and so on. A total of 12.75 miles is covered, 5.75 of which are run at a good speed. This type of workout is known as a ladder, with a progression of intervals of different distance. Other routines may simply repeat the same distance a specified number of times with a standard walking or jogging period between: 24×220; 220 jog in between, for example. Still others may run a series of sets of the same distance, as in 6×220, jog 880; 6×220, jog 880; 6×220, jog 880; 6×220, jog 880.

There are many variables that can be shifted about in interval workouts, though it is questionable how much difference they really make, given the same general level of effort. Many interval theorists claim that it is the recovery period that is most important. Certainly the level of effort put into each interval is important. Not all of them can be run at absolutely top speed. One way to keep the difficulty of the workout high (therefore presumably providing a lot of stimulation) without burning the legs out is to keep the rest jogs short, as in the ladder workout. The 220 rests don't give the body enough time to recover from oxygen debt, so speed is kept at a moderate level.

Assuming the body is stressed about the same amount, it probably doesn't matter a whole lot whether you run a ladder like the one above or some other workout, like 20×440. A mixture may provide the most balanced training, physically and psychologically, but it is doubtful whether it matters if you mix your distances every day or from one workout to the next. The function of intervals within the total framework of a runner's training (discussed later) is the important thing to understand.

Distance Training

The idea of extensive distance training at relatively low speeds has been discussed elsewhere in this book. Basically, this type of training is intended to build endurance, aerobic capacity, and physical and psychological tolerance for extended exercise. Van Aaken theorizes that it teaches the body to operate by metabolizing fats. Certainly, it helps to control weight and builds physical reserves that can later be called on during interval sessions, strength and speed workouts, and races.

One important feature of distance work is the weekly long run, usually run at relatively slow speeds but extended enough to simulate the depletion of glycogen and liquid reserves that occurs in long races. The marathoner typically might run thirty miles. Intermediate runners and racers training for shorter distances might run twenty or twenty-five miles.

The importance of distance seems to be one of the few incontrovertible conclusions that can be drawn from modern training. It is the major difference between modern training and that of the past. Although it does not follow that more distance is *always* better, few top-level runners cover less than a hundred miles a week, and averages in the neighborhood of 140–150 miles are quite common among the best runners.

Distance training can also be run at moderate or fast speeds, of course, and many runners do much of their distance training at a pace approaching the maximum they can manage, perhaps thirty seconds slower per mile than their best time for the distance being covered. The arguments for this type of training are fairly obvious. It is more consistent with the generally accepted theory that training should be specific. You don't train primarily with chin-ups to run the hundred-yard dash, so if you want to run fast, why train slowly?

Neither fast nor slow distance needs to be exclusive, since there is obviously a continuum of speeds between. It is also clear

that what is slow for one runner may be fast for another. Many runners run some of their mileage at comparatively slow speeds and
some at near-racing speed.

Tempo running is a term that can have different meanings, but
it usually refers to running at racing speed, partly for the purpose
of learning the proper pace. Tempo running can serve to teach the
body what the proper pace feels like. (The importance of pacing
was discussed in the last chapter.) It also provides a test by which
the runner can judge how appropriate a particular pace is. Many
slow-distance advocates, following Dr. van Aaken, believe in working one tempo interval into each day's distance workout. This
serves the function both of maintaining speed and embedding the
feel of a particular pace in the mind and body.

Mileage, Collapse Point, and Time Lag

Several of the theories propounded by ultramarathoner Ken
Young, discussed earlier on pp. 123–24, are particularly relevant
to anyone training to run a race over any of the longer distances.
To iterate briefly, Young associates the common phenomenon of
hitting the wall—a sudden and radical slowing in the latter stages
of a race—with a specific "collapse point," which is determined
primarily by the training mileage that the runner has accumulated
during the preceding months. Young maintains that the most important contributing factor is not the longest individual runs but
the cumulative distance covered over long periods. His calculation
of the collapse point is to divide the total mileage of the longest two
consecutive recent months by twenty, yielding the longest distance
a runner can expect to manage before hitting the wall.

Young, who has held several American track records at distances beyond the marathon, feels that the phenomenon of hitting
the wall is associated with the depletion of the glycogen stored in
the muscles. After the runner has used up this glycogen supply,
running can be continued only by metabolizing fats, a process that
yields energy at a slower rate. (The fats used are fatty acids that are
metabolically active, not a spare tire carried around the middle.)
By running longer distances regularly, you increase your glycogen
storage capacity. This theory explains why so many runners who
average six or seven miles a day hit the wall at about twenty miles

in the marathon. (Remember that if you run ten miles a day five days a week, you are only averaging seven miles a day.)

If you combine the long period that Young feels is necessary to raise your collapse point with the requirement that mileage be increased slowly to avoid overstress injuries, you will see that a long time is required to build up properly for longer races. I recommend increasing average mileage no more than 10 percent each week, and Young's two-month estimate for a training effect from higher mileages has been borne out by the experience of many runners.

To give a practical illustration, suppose you are currently running thirty-five miles per week and you want to build up to a point where you can run a marathon at your normal speed without hitting the wall. To raise your collapse point to twenty-six miles, you need to put in sixty-one miles per week. It will take six weeks to get your mileage up to that figure by raising it 10 percent each week, assuming that you have no problems that force you to reduce the rate of increase. You will then need to run at that level for another two months to bring your collapse point to the desired level. Thus, three and a half months of training *at a minimum* are needed just to acquire proper endurance.

Fartlek

Fartlek, which means "speed play" in Swedish, is a sort of free-form interval training that is integrated into normal distance work on the roads or trails. The runner plays freely with the pace while running, rather than falling into a constant rote pattern. He or she explores many paces, now accelerating on a hill, now running at top speed for a mile, now jogging for a while, now doing a series of sprints. The amount of effort expended in a workout is determined by the runner's mood for the day and the feeling of the body. Clearly, if it is run in the proper spirit, fartlek can be as effective as interval work—and a lot more enjoyable. It is particularly effective when running trails, since work at various speeds can be mixed with the varying demands of hills and curves.

The disadvantage of fartlek is that it is less controlled than interval work, less amenable to measurement when one is trying to improve speed. Although fartlek is more pleasant than interval work and can be just as demanding, it can also permit you to delude yourself into thinking you are working harder than you really are. Many runners like to alternate fartlek workouts with interval ones during their period of speed work, thus combining the less boring fartlek training with the more controlled routine of intervals.

Another mixture is used by some runners who don't have a track easily available or who hate the track so much that they never run on one when it can be avoided. Intervals can be run along a road or trail either in exact measured groups taped out beforehand or in regular patterns with only a few measured lengths for timing purposes. Such mixtures can range between fartlek training and formal intervals run on the road.

Hill Training

Hill training is another idea that has been around for a long time, though it has been advocated in more specific form and for more specific purposes by modern coaches like Arthur Lydiard and Percy Cerutty. Hill training is naturally included in hilly cross-country courses and trail runs.

Like intervals, hills can be run in many ways when used specifically for training. One can run up very long hills (if they exist where you live), which may be steep or gradual. For example, you might run up a mountain road or trail that gains several thousand feet. Clearly, on a long hill like this the overall pace must be nearly aerobic; otherwise, you would grind to a halt after a mile or so. Variations in the grade or the pace can mix aerobic and anaerobic running while keeping the demand at a fairly high level.

Short hills are usually run as fast as possible so that a considerable oxygen debt is built up, as it is in interval training. This sort of training may be done during continuous running on rolling trails or roads, with the downhill and level portions providing the recoveries, or it may be done up and down a single hill. Lydiard advocates bounding up a medium-length hill (about half a mile), springing high at each step, and then running back down as fast as possible. He then has his runners do a recovery jog, follows with some hard striding on the flats, and then repeats the whole routine. Cerutty liked to have his runners sprint at full speed up sand dunes.

Any kind of hill running is excellent for cardiopulmonary training, hill technique, psychological toughening, and most of all for strength. To run up a hill, you must drive harder with your legs to lift your body weight as well as propel it forward, so the leg muscles are bound to be strengthened. It is a form of resistance exercise; as with weight lifting, the muscles are pushing against greater resistance than usual, so they become stronger. On steep hills the quadriceps muscles are used more extensively than they are in level running.

Putting It Together

The problem for any runner is not in finding ingredients for his or her training but in combining them in a sensible fashion. There should be a rationale behind your training. You should know

Hill training is one of the best methods for building strength and anaerobic capacity. Running hilly trails is one of the most pleasant kinds of hill training.

what you are doing and why, and if something doesn't work, you should change the routine in a responsive way, not just at random. Keep a record of what you do over the years. Learn what works and what does not. Don't make sudden shifts unless injury calls for reducing the load. Move into new routines gradually. The importance of shifting to higher mileage at a moderate rate has been mentioned before. If you are working toward a marathon, it is not going to do you any good to go from seventy to a hundred miles per week one month before the race. You're more likely to lose the conditioning you've built up than to improve it.

The training system that makes the most sense to me is the one advocated by former U.S. Olympian Ron Daws, which he adapted from the ideas of Arthur Lydiard. Basically, Daws maintains that most of the runner's training should be distance running on the roads. Speeds will naturally vary with the individual, but Lydiard seems to advocate maintaining speeds close to one's maximum aerobic pace, so that over the months the pace can be expected to increase gradually. Much of this question of speed is a matter of emphasis, and it is important not to push too hard all the time. The principles of avoiding overstressing that have been repeated throughout this book should be followed. Daws emphasizes that during this endurance-building distance phase, training for speed will do no good and may well cause injury or interfere with the goal of building reserves. The important point is that though one should not merely jog slowly along, the primary ingredient at this stage is distance, not speed.

If you are aiming at a specific race or season, this phase should have a planned length. It should certainly last a minimum of several months, even for the experienced runner. For the beginner or intermediate, it may go on for much longer, until the basic endurance and fitness necessary to sustain speed work have been acquired.

Daws and Lydiard advocate moving from this stamina-building phase to hill running, which gives the runner strength and initiates anaerobic training. The Lydiard-style hill training has already been described. Different runners pursue their own variations, but the crucial ingredient is hard running up hills, whether done with bounds or not and whether done by continuous trail running or by repeated intervals up a single hill. From the point of view of learning hill technique, it is also important to incorporate some hard

Extensive distance running at aerobic speeds builds the endurance necessary for other phases of training.

downhill running. Hill training should be mixed in with distance running on the hard–easy pattern discussed in more detail below. As with everything else, work into your hill training slowly, to give your muscles and tendons a chance to adjust themselves to the new loads. Concentrated hill training on this plan generally lasts a month or a little longer, though occasional hill workouts may be interspersed into later phases of training as well.

Following hill training, Lydiard and Daws use a "sharpening" phase of interval and speed work to bring the runner into racing shape. The idea is to build up one's speed to racing level gradually over a period of perhaps a couple of months, peaking at whatever time one wants to perform at the best level. During this period, each week will probably include a couple of tough interval workouts and some fartlek, interspersed with moderate distance runs and one long run.

The exact scheduling of intervals during this period is a matter of finding out what works for you, but it is important not to try to push up the speed too soon. Both from a physical and psychological point of view, trying immediately for maximum speed tends to burn you out. Don't even take a watch along during the first couple of weeks of interval training. Your times at this stage will be disappointing, and you will be too tempted to try to force them up prematurely. Work hard, but don't use yourself up. At the end of a month of sharpening, you should really begin to speed up. Then start working for time, but gear your best performances toward the competition you're shooting for. Feel out your own best schedule. Naturally fast runners may be able to move very quickly from slow distance to peak performance. Others need at least a couple of months to work up.

Daws's book, *The Self-Made Olympian*, is one of the best running autobiographies around—witty, restrained, good humored, and inspiring. It also includes some of the most cogent training advice available, especially on scheduling and interval training. Anyone who is getting into racing seriously should read it, and it is recommended to all runners.

The Work Load

The level of training that the body needs and the quantity it can stand are among the most individual of traits. This is one important reason to develop your own schedule, rather than trying to copy someone else's. Very few individuals, however, can tolerate uniformly hard training. No matter how good you get, there are limits to the amount of stress your body will tolerate without breaking down. If you push too fast, you'll be able to exceed those limits without noticing and thus stand a good chance of really hurting yourself.

Training should therefore be based on some kind of rhythm that is in tune with *your* body. Bill Bowerman's hard–easy approach works well for many people and is a good basic routine to experiment with while you find your own patterns. The idea is simply to follow each hard day with an easy one. This approach is adaptable to runners at all levels of training. If you take your first twenty-mile run on Sunday, don't plan on another long one Monday; stick to a distance and speed that are moderate for you. Don't try to run sharp interval sessions back to back—keep them separated by a day or two of easy distance.

It is important not to let your ego become involved in your judgment of the proper rhythm of hard and easy days in your training schedule. Steve Prefontaine, who before his accidental death was one of the best distance runners in the world, needed two easy days between hard workouts. He was intelligent enough to take them. Some runners are tough enough to do a couple of days of hard workouts in between easy days. You have to feel your own way into the best training routine for you. It is best to start with at least one easy day after each hard workout, however. If you are still yearning for more after a few months of serious training on that schedule, try an occasional back-to-back workout. Remember, though, that some of the tough runners who have run hard almost every day have eventually been badly hurt. Take the long view.

Heat Acclimatization

Dissipation of heat from the body is one of the most significant factors for the racer, particularly at high ambient temperatures and during long races. Dehydration and heat buildup can be major factors in lowering the performance of the runner even in distance races when the temperature is in the fifties. The danger of long races in hot weather, particularly when evaporation from the skin is reduced by high humidity, has been pointed out previously. Anyone planning to run races in hot weather needs to acclimatize to heat beforehand, both to improve performance and to increase the safety margin against heat exhaustion and stroke.

No matter how well acclimatized you are, heat is bound to affect your performance. Records are almost never set in distance events when the weather is warm. You should recognize this in planning your strategy for a race. Heat will affect everyone else's running too, and if you have acclimatized while others have not, you will have a distinct advantage. You will also suffer a lot less after the race. I ran my first marathon in fairly humid weather, with the temperature at 85°, and I was not heat acclimatized. My muscles were so stiff afterward that I couldn't walk normally for days. I still came off a lot better than many other runners, however. Quite a few passed out, and many required medical treatment.

The acclimatized runner perspires more so that less blood is required to circulate in the skin for cooling. More blood is then available to carry oxygen to the muscles. (It follows from this that depriving yourself of fluids is not one of the things you want to do while training to perform better in the heat. You can maintain good perspiration only if you have sufficient liquid intake.) The concentration of electrolytes in the perspiration is also greatly reduced. Effectively, your sweat becomes much more diluted as you acclimatize. The runner's body also drains most of its cooling fluid from the tissues, not from the blood supply. The acclimatized person may stop running efficiently when excessive fluid loss has occurred, but he or she will not pass out or go into shock.

The way to acclimatize is simple enough: run in the heat. Run when it is unpleasantly hot and the sweat pours off into your eyes. Get plenty to drink and don't try to go too fast, but run when it is hot enough to be uncomfortable three times a week for about six weeks before the first race that may occur in hot weather. Run in the afternoon instead of the morning. If the weather isn't hot enough, just add more clothes instead of taking them off. Some runners who are heat acclimatizing where spring weather is chilly train wearing four or five sweat suits to prepare for a possible hot-weather marathon like Boston.

12/ *Running a Marathon*

Why do people run marathons? Even the distance is irrational: 26 miles, 385 yards, a monument to a particular course that was set up in England for the Olympics and lengthened so it would extend to the royal palace. It is hard to defend a claim that anybody runs marathons for fun. A ten- or fifteen-mile race can be enjoyed physically, but it is practically impossible to give a marathon one's best without suffering a good deal over the last few miles. The traditional expression of this fact is the statement that the halfway mark in a marathon is at twenty miles. Marathoning definitely stresses the body beyond its reasonable capacity. You may train every day to make yourself healthier, but after a marathon you're debilitated, and it takes time to recover: you can run only a few a year at maximum effort. Why then has the marathon become *the* premier distance race, attracting incredible numbers of runners every year and commanding attention that is given to no other distance?

Certainly there are almost as many reasons for running marathons as there are participants in the races that have sprung up from New York to Seaside, Oregon. Perhaps the oddity of the distance appeals to the sometimes unconventional personalities who take up running in the first place. The physical challenge of the race is certainly one of its attractions, whether the individual marathoner is a world-class distance runner moving at a five-minute-per-mile pace, or a former cardiac patient trying to finish in six hours. The challenge is greater because of the unpredictability of the distance. The veteran racer starts most distances *knowing* within a close margin how fast he or she will run, and usually the mental prediction is fairly accurate. Very few runners, even the

The Boston Marathon is the nation's oldest. The spectators lining the entire twenty-six-mile course are one reason that Boston is America's classic road race.

best, can run a marathon as consistently as they can run five, ten, or even twenty miles. Marathons are full of surprises.

The marathon has the special appeal of long tradition, a mythology of its own, a legacy of countless tales of agony, triumph, and whimsy. America's classic distance race, Boston, is a marathon. Every modern Olympics has had one. There may be better distances, but none has the romance and special mystique of the marathon.

Running the marathon has become something of a distance runner's rite of passage, the traditional initiation into the tribe of confirmed road runners. When you begin jogging around the block, the thought of going over 26 miles seems absurd. Then, as your training mileage increases, the possibility of actually running the distance of a marathon starts to creep into your mind. Finally, if you are like many distance runners, you begin to train for a marathon just to run one, to find out whether you can do it. Many people run a marathon as their first race, because they are more interested in experiencing the distance than in racing per se. (It's important to note that there is a difference between running the distance at the best pace you can, as you attempt to do in a marathon or any other race, and running it at training speeds. You may choose to run twenty-six miles a number of times before attempting to do so in a race.)

The First One

There is a common set of errors that most people seem to repeat when they run their first marathons. Few of us are able to avoid this beginner's syndrome altogether, though some of us fall into the trap harder than others. Many people don't finish their first attempt, others have to do a lot of walking toward the end, and most of the remaining novices finish very slowly because they ran too fast during the early stages of the race.

The first big mistake is to start running too fast. There is an incredible euphoria that takes over at the beginning of a marathon, whether it is a big one such as Boston with thousands of runners hopping up and down, waiting for the crowd in front to thin enough so that they can start to run, or a smaller local run with fewer than a hundred participants. You probably won't even realize how fast you are going. The pace seems absurdly easy. I remember my first marathon, on a hot, humid day for which I wasn't at all acclimatized; I loped along easily at what seemed a relaxed tempo. I was actually running 6:10 miles when I should have been doing 7:20s. Even if you do realize how fast you're going, you are likely to delude yourself into thinking that you can keep it up. There are all sorts of rationalizations that your excited and slightly oxygen-starved mind can dream up during those first ten miles. Sometime after that, however—the exact location depends on how badly you've been deceiving yourself—you begin to feel the awful truth in your legs. The majority of reasonably well-trained novice runners start to falter between sixteen and twenty miles and either drop to half their previous speed or quit altogether.

With proper training and mental discipline, you can avoid all the standard mistakes, or at least mitigate the consequences so that you pass most of the walking wounded, rather than having them pass you. Your first marathon still won't be easy; the last five or six miles will be hard and painful, but you will at least run the course in a time that reflects your training and potential, rather than crashing into the wall or tearing a muscle at the eighteen-mile mark. A few general rules follow, and then some suggestions about training for a first marathon.

Getting Ready for Your First Marathon

1. Decide on a realistic goal for a first marathon, in terms of the date you want to run one and what sort of time you would like to run it in. Don't get your heart so set on a certain speed or race that you won't get any satisfaction if you have to make later revisions. Above all, allow yourself enough time to train before the race. This period is discussed below, but it should nearly always last a minimum of three months, and often much longer.

2. Try to pick a good race, one that does not have an extremely difficult course and that is not usually during excessively hot weather. If you want to run your marathon in the heat or on a hilly route, plan to do the special training that these require. Races such as Boston have fine, cool weather some years, but they can be very hot. If you plan to run one of these, you have to train for the heat. Most important are plenty of watering stations and accurate mileage markers. You can't check your pace without accurate distances. Timers are nice, though you can wear a watch. If the course doesn't have markers, plan to drive it beforehand in a car with a calibrated odometer so that you can figure out your own pacing.

3. Plan your training schedule between now and the time of the race, and then stick to it. Recognize that if you slack off or get sick for any length of time, you'll probably have to change your plans and run a later race. You'll find that the training has amazing effects on your conditioning, but it can't be rushed.

4. Plan to taper off a little a couple of weeks before the marathon. It is a time for rest and fine tuning—it's too late to get in any basic conditioning. Never increase your mileage to new highs at this stage; you'll only sap your reserves. Plan to use this time for some speed work, if you are strong enough, and for practicing the pace you want to run in the race. Don't stop running, but don't put in brutal workouts. This is the time when enthusiasm frequently gets the better of common sense. Many people put in their first hundred-mile weeks just before they plan to run their marathons. Avoid this trap.

5. Know the course, if you possibly can. Don't believe the advance propaganda. You might want to run it fresh, but there is definitely an advantage in riding over it in a car beforehand, or, better yet, on a bicycle. If there are five miles of tough hills at the

Age is rarely a barrier in running. This young competitor is a veteran of several marathons.

end, it helps a lot to save some energy for them. It helps even more to know they are there so that they don't destroy you psychologically when you reach them.

6. Figure out your pacing in advance, carefully and realistically. You should at least be able to run ten miles fairly comfortably at the pace you choose. If you are running the marathon on training that averages fewer than sixty miles a week, so that you can be sure of hitting the wall, plan to run slower than your ten-mile pace so that you can prolong the collapse point as much as possible. (Thirty seconds slower per mile than you can run ten miles is a good figure.)

7. Don't eat a lot before the race (I prefer nothing), get lots of liquids, and make a bowel movement before the race. Run in a combination of shoes and socks that you know are comfortable for long distances, not in brand-new racing shoes. Make sure you have clothes that are warm enough in case you need them and that give adequate sun protection if you need that. Lubricate points of possible chafing beforehand with petroleum jelly. Cover any spots where you tend to get blisters with adhesive tape or moleskin. Some people have trouble with blisters on their feet, and many women need to tape under the fastenings and the lower front band of their bras.

Training

If your goal is to run a marathon, you have to plan your training to lead up to it, unless you are already running an average of at least ten miles a day. One advantage to planning your training well is that it forces you to think realistically about the rate of progress you can expect.

The first question you need to answer is how you want to run the marathon. Is your goal simply to finish, or do you have some time in mind? Either objective is equally valid, but the training implications can be very different. If finishing is what is really important to you—perhaps in four, five, or six hours—then you might reasonably decide that you could be satisfied with forty or fifty miles of training a week. If, on the other hand, you have a time objective, perhaps three or three and a half hours, it is important to run enough miles in training to extend your collapse point at least to the distance of the race, requiring at least sixty miles a week for a couple of consecutive months. When I started thinking about a marathon, I decided I wanted to run one when I could plan on taking no more than twice as long as Bill Rodgers and Frank Shorter, say four hours and fifteen minutes. By the time I actually started training for a specific race, I had set my goals a little higher and would not really have been happy with a time over three and a half hours. All that matters is that your training be commensurate with your expectations.

The first thing to remember in planning your training is Ken Young's rule that your collapse point (in the best circumstances) will be a twentieth of the mileage total during your longest consecutive sixty days of recent training. To bring your collapse point up to the length of a marathon, you must therefore run 524 miles in two consecutive months prior to your race. You also need some time between this conditioning period and the actual marathon, so a minimum of ten weeks' training will be required for this phase, even if you are already running fairly high mileage. It is not a good idea to throw yourself immediately into this nine- or ten-mile-a-day schedule if you are currently running five or six, however. If you do, you'll probably come down with a nasty injury after a couple of weeks, and you'll have to start from an even lower level of fitness after you recover. The rule of thumb is to add an average of not more than 10 percent to your weekly mileage.

Suppose that you are now running about forty miles a week. This is probably enough to allow you to finish a marathon if you pace yourself well, running at a moderate pace for the first fifteen miles or so and dropping to a slow, painful jog when the glycogen depletion catches up with you. If you try this, be sure to pace yourself slowly, though; if you try to run fast, you are unlikely to finish at all.

If you'd like to run a faster marathon, you might set up a schedule this way:

First week: 44 miles   Sixth through thirteenth weeks:
Second week: 48 miles   70 miles per week
Third week: 53 miles   Fourteenth week: Easy prior to
Fourth week: 58 miles   marathon
Fifth week: 64 miles

This schedule would allow a little over three months of training prior to the marathon and would assure you that your collapse point (thirty miles) would be well over the distance of the race. The beginning buildup is at approximately 10 percent a week. A more serious runner might want a longer buildup and a higher weekly mileage to allow the body to acquire greater reserves.

Within the schedule, there are important variations as well. The exact mileage does not need to be followed rigidly, provided the general range is correct. It would make no difference if you ran sixty miles the third week and only fifty-five the fourth. It is the overall pattern that counts. You should try to run every day, but most of us miss some occasionally. You should take some long runs, usually on weekends, to accustom your body to extended effort. Don't try to run fast on your long days. The long days will normally make up for the mileage you lose on occasional short days or missed workouts.

Remember to use some kind of hard–easy pattern. Don't try to run hard all the time, especially when you are building up mileage. Intervals, hill workouts, and speed work all have their place, but this place is *after* you have achieved your basic fitness. Adding distance and increasing speed both place a lot of stress on your joints, muscles, and tendons. Don't try to do everything at once. Building up your endurance will naturally add some speed, and if you feel good during the weeks after you have leveled off at seventy miles, you can put some speed training into your workouts, but don't overdo it. If you really want to do a lot of speed work, you probably need to lengthen your training period to allow for it.

Your exact routine will depend on your own preferences and schedule, but in the early part of the seventy-mile period, it might look like this:

MONDAY	TUESDAY	WEDNESDAY	THURSDAY	FRIDAY
10 miles moderate effort	7 miles easy	11 miles fairly hard	8 miles easy	10 miles moderate effort

SATURDAY	SUNDAY
16 miles slow	9 miles easy

Later on, you might want to work in some intervals on one or two days, followed by easy days, and lengthen the long run. If you are running more than sixty miles a week, I think it is a good idea to do at least one run of marathon length before the race. You may finish it going very slowly, but you'll then *know* you can handle the distance and be able to concentrate on pacing. Do it at least a month before the race.

Runners who are concerned with better times should work up to 70–100 miles a week well before the race, giving their bodies time to stabilize at this level for several months. They should then begin doing hill workouts, and finally, during the last month or two before the race, should begin sharpening with intervals.

A typical workout for a good runner a month before a marathon might go like this:

MONDAY	TUESDAY	WEDNESDAY	THURSDAY	FRIDAY
AM: 9 miles easy	14 miles, moderate effort	2-mile warm-up 10 miles intervals 1 mile jog	10 miles easy	AM: 9 miles, moderate
PM: 5 miles hard				PM: 5-mile hill workout

SATURDAY	SUNDAY
13 miles, moderate	25-mile run

The total for the week is 103 miles, with a good mixture of work. Splitting the day's running into two segments is good, if you can work it into your schedule. There are no magic formulas, however, and the workouts listed here are just examples. You have to make up your own schedules to fit the time you have available. Keep a record and pay attention to the way your body reacts, to find out what works best. Remember, though, to leave the speed work alone until you have achieved good fitness.

Strategy

Regardless of whether you are running your marathon just to finish, to cross the line in a particular time, or to beat some other runner, you must plan the race and pay attention to your performance all the way through. The typical mistake of going out too fast has been mentioned before, but it can't be overemphasized. Nearly every novice tends to do it. Work on your pace the week before the race, running a measured course of a mile or so at exactly the rate you want to run the marathon. If your normal training pace is 8½ minutes per mile and you run 70 miles a week, 8 minutes per mile might be a reasonable pace for the marathon, for a total of 3½ hours. If most of your training is at 7-minute miles, you might reasonably set a 6½-minute pace for your first marathon. Entry information usually specifies where mileage markers are and whether splits are given. (Splits are times called out by an official at a particular mileage.) A well-run marathon might have splits at one mile and at each five-mile interval.

In your training you should pay careful attention to the feel of your proper pace. How hard do you breathe? How fast are your legs moving? How much are you stretching? Memorize the rhythm. In the first minutes of the marathon, concentrate on that feeling and lock into your pace. Check it at the first split, and adjust it if necessary. Don't worry about tactics on your first attempt at the distance. Try to run an evenly paced race, which is physiologically most efficient. Pay attention to the pace and to your body. If you lose concentration, you are likely either to slow down or to start going too fast. After a few miles, when you're firmly locked into your pace, you might want to socialize with someone going the right speed, but be careful not to get off your own stride.

Keeping your liquid intake up is one of the most important things you can do during a marathon. Get plenty to drink before the race starts, and drink as often as possible during the race. Dehydration is one of the most important limiting factors for the distance runner in races of marathon length, even when the weather is not hot or humid. In these conditions a good intake of liquid is essential to avoid injury as well as to insure good performance. Electrolyte replacement drinks are fine, though it is best not to try strange ones during a race. Plain water will do perfectly well if you have acclimatized to the temperatures you are running in. Though you cannot absorb enough liquid to make up for what you are losing during a run, excessive drinking is rarely a problem. Drinking too little is common. If the race does not have enough aid stations, try to arrange your own liquid supplies, either by having someone supply you at prearranged spots along the course or by leaving cached water bottles yourself.

Running the Race

The routine you follow immediately prior to the marathon probably doesn't matter a great deal, as long as you don't have to make an extended bathroom stop during the race. Warming up somewhat is generally a good idea, unless the day is hot. Stretching is helpful and gives you something to do during the nervous period prior to a race, along with checking the knots in your shoelaces and similar rituals.

If the field is large, don't push up to the front with the top racers, even if you will be held up for a couple of minutes by moving back into the main throng of runners. Try to position yourself with the runners of approximately your own level of ability, so that as the field sorts itself out during the first few minutes of the race you are neither blocking faster runners behind nor forced to work past a large number of slower runners in front. In smaller races this problem doesn't present itself.

The start of a marathon is exciting; it is the release of all that energy you have been storing up over the months of training. You won't have any trouble getting started here, even if you are somewhat anxious. Almost everyone has a good time, and there is a lot of chatting and joking. Just remember to pay attention to your pace.

For the next ten or fifteen miles, the race is usually easy and very pleasant. This is the time to enjoy the company of the other runners, the character of the course, and the scenery. Take the time to keep your pace where it should be, particularly on the hills, if there are any. Don't slow too much on the upgrades, but avoid really attacking the hills on your first marathon; they can eat up a lot of energy. Make up some of your time on the downhills, but beware of getting a stitch while you are running downhill. Deep belly breathing helps to prevent this.

During the last five or ten miles you'll encounter the major challenge of the marathon. If you are short on training, have run too fast, or aren't properly acclimatized, you may have to use every ounce of willpower just to keep going. Even if you are still running properly, you will find that fatigue and aching muscles set in here, and you'll have to use all your concentration to maintain your pace. If your attention wanders, you'll slow down. Keep your movements fluid and your body relaxed. Run as efficiently as possible. It is in those last few miles that you will have a chance to test yourself against the experience of the marathon. There is not much talking anymore; each runner is busy in his or her own mind finding the reserves to keep going. Each mile seems to go on forever.

The finish is a moment to be savored, the end of a long pilgrimage. No matter how bone tired you are, no matter how your legs ache, the satisfaction is enormous and somehow worth the sacrifice. Whether your time is below three hours or in excess of six, there is a special personal triumph. Enjoy it; you've earned it!

13/ *Running for a Lifetime*

One of the features of running that is particularly satisfying is that you can keep running throughout your life, barring some catastrophic event. The likelihood of such an event is even reduced by the fact of your running, and your life expectancy may be increased as well. The improvement of quality is surely more important than effects on the span of life, however. If you can retain your vitality, alertness, and enjoyment of each day throughout your life, an increase of a few years in its duration is only a secondary benefit.

The tremendous growth of running among people over forty is one of the most impressive aspects of the running movement. Hundreds of thousands of people who had begun to feel the physical effects of middle age creeping up on them have found that they can feel healthier and more vital than they did when they were twenty. How many members of the population can keep up with old John Kelley, who ran his forty-sixth Boston Marathon in three and a half hours just five months before his seventieth birthday? He is a man sparkling with life; he paints with oils at his retirement home on Cape Cod after going for his daily early morning run, and he seems to enjoy every minute of the day.

One of the indisputable benefits of regular running is that it slows down many of the effects of aging. A number of studies have indicated that at least some of the important forms of physical deterioration that take place with increasing age are radically reduced by regular exercise. Maximum oxygen uptake (which measures aerobic power) declines inexorably as you get older, given a particular level of activity. However, it declines much more slowly if you run regularly, and because a runner has far better aerobic capacity than the average person, a runner in his sixties may frequently have an oxygen uptake that is higher than that of the average man in his twenties. No one knows how continuous athletic training affects most of the changes commonly associated with aging. Since most adults in America become generally inactive by their twenties, if not sooner, it is difficult to separate those effects that are a result of inactivity from those that are truly a result of aging. One can speculate, but not enough study has been done to yield any definitive answers. This is true partly because physicians have only recently interested themselves in the physiology of people who stay fit and active.

Aging and the Athlete

There is no question that the body's capacity for maximal physical performance declines with age. John Kelley now takes an hour longer to run the course from Hopkinton to Boston than he did when he won the marathons in 1935 and 1945. Some physical parameters seem to decline inescapably, regardless of training. Maximal heart rate is an example; it falls at a steady rate of a little less than a beat each year whether you run races or sit in front of the television. Other capacities decline inexorably too, but the rate of decline may be greatly reduced by exercise and such other factors as diet. Muscle strength probably falls into this category. Still

Running can be taken up by a healthy individual at any age. Keeping it up slows many of the effects of aging.

other changes for the worse that are normally listed as characteristics of aging, such as increased body fat, are in fact completely
controllable. Reduction in muscle mass and weakening of bones are
at least slowed by exercise and may be halted.

The possible athletic performances for the runner are bound
to decline over the years, but this is no reason for a lack of interest
in achieving a high level of performance. There are now age-group
championships, age records, age divisions in races, and elaborate
tables that show the relative merits of various times in most standard racing lengths between people of different ages. The runner
can work not only to improve his or her best performance but also
the relative levels from one year to the next. Some runners now
look forward to their fortieth birthday so that they can start competing in masters' events.

Age group and division racing have already been discussed.
Apart from these methods of letting older runners compete with
one another, the statistics compiled by Ken Young of the National
Running Data Center permit detailed comparison of people of different ages in different events. Young has extrapolated from the
age-group records for each distance to provide a table of relative
performances, using a point system. The best performances receive
one thousand points, and by checking the charts a runner can compare his or her performance with world records or with other
times. In the marathon, for example, a sixty-year-old man who
runs a 2:42 marathon has surpassed the world-record level of a
younger man running 2:08. A set of these tables can be found in
the booklet *Age of the Runner*. Such statistics will be imperfect for
a number of years, of course, until older competitors have raced
long enough to give us a more realistic view of their capacities. For
women, it is scarcely even possible to begin compiling them. We
don't have an idea how fast a thirty-year-old woman marathoner
can run, never mind being able to compare her performance with
that of a female runner who is sixty-five.

The very uncertainty of all this information is one of the exciting areas of exploration for us all. How fast can people run when
they are seventy? We will find out. As we begin to see runners
who have competed steadily through many years, our understanding will begin to grow. Until then, we have the inspiration of
the John Kelleys to hint at the possibilities.

Most of us (those who don't come from a background of running) have our own special horizons to explore as well. Although my own level of possible performance continues to decline, my actual performances are continuing to improve. I can run a lot faster and farther now than when I was twenty. For the middle-aged beginner, there is a long way to go before he or she has to begin to worry about the limitations imposed by aging. When those limits are finally approached, that in itself can provide major satisfaction, because it means that you are somewhere near the best condition *you* can be in. And after that point, if you ever reach it, it is still possible to continue to improve your relative condition by comparing your performances through age-corrected charts with your times in past races.

The Question of Running, Longevity, and Heart Attacks

Will running enable you to live longer? The answer to this question is the subject of major controversy among some members of the medical profession. There have been many claims for running in this respect, but currently the hottest debate centers around the question of whether running helps prevent heart attacks. Tom Bassler, M.D., on the one hand, maintains that anyone who has finished a marathon and continues to live the "marathon life-style" (moderate eating, no smoking, and regular running) is *immune* from heart attacks (myocardial infarction). Other physicians specializing in the causes of coronary heart disease assert that running can be dangerous for those who are prone to heart attacks and that it has no prophylactic value whatever. There have been dozens of studies trying to determine the effect of exercise on coronary risk, and the debate over their conclusions goes on.

There is less dispute among runners. The great majority of runners seem to believe that running will help them live longer and that if it does not make them immune to heart attacks, it at least vastly lowers the probability of their occurrence. Even those scientifically oriented runners who do not believe that the case for immunity has been proven are usually of the opinion that running has a preventive influence.

The difficulty of proving that running or exercise in general helps to prevent heart attacks or of relating exercise to coronary heart disease in any way is that there are so many other variables involved, many of which may be associated with running. It can be demonstrated that statistically a regular runner who is slim, doesn't smoke, doesn't consume too many fats, and manages to relax away the daily buildup of psychological tension, perhaps during a run, is far less likely to have a heart attack (and quite a few other serious diseases) than someone who never gets any exercise, is overweight, smokes, and worries a lot. With the possible exception of tension and worry, there is a clear association between all these characteristics. Runners don't smoke, are slimmer than the general run of the population, and consume less excess fat. You can also certainly demonstrate that running causes a loss in body fat and associated characteristics in the sense that it consumes calories.

A scientist can object, however, that there is self-selection by runners—that the healthy person chooses running rather than the running generating health. Does running make people slim and less prone to heart attacks, or do people choose to run because they are naturally more active, slimmer, and less prone to heart attacks? This is the kind of objection that has been raised to most of the studies used to try to demonstrate the value of exercise in preventing heart attacks.

For example, there was a famous study done in Britain of the rate of heart disease among drivers and conductors on London's double-decker buses. The drivers sit and drive all day while the conductors walk around, scurry up and down between the decks, jump down onto the sidewalk, and run and leap back up after the bus starts moving. Naturally, the conductors have fewer heart attacks. However, the skeptic must ask, are the conductors slimmer and do they have fewer heart attacks because they get more exercise, or do they choose their jobs and the drivers choose theirs because the conductors are naturally slimmer, more active, and less prone to heart attacks? One can construct plausible models and theories to argue for several possible relationships between the variables. And because people are individuals who make their own choices, because there are so many variables, and because it takes such a long time for results to show, it is impossible to prove any of these arguments scientifically. At this time it is also impossible to demonstrate statistically that running and jogging help prevent cardiovascular disease, because not enough people have done it for a

Though running probably allows you to live longer, what is really important is that it allows you to live better. Keep it up!

long enough period to permit valid conclusions. This is especially the case with marathoners.

It is quite possible to show that a person who runs a lot and has all the usual attributes of a runner does have a lot fewer risk factors for heart attacks and a number of other degenerative diseases than the average person. Furthermore, since many people have done so, it is demonstrably possible for a person to lose weight, become fitter, and maintain good physical condition by getting into the habit of running.

Furthermore, runners' bodies tell them that they are feeling better, that their health has improved, and that they are enjoying life more as a result of regular exercise. These data cannot be used as scientific proof, but they provide more than adequate evidence for personal decisions. It really doesn't matter whether you can prove scientifically that you will live longer by running. It is a reasonable assumption from your own experience. Personally, it is even irrelevant to me whether I will live longer because I run. It gives me enough pleasure and improves the quality of my life such that I would keep it up even if someone could prove to me that it would make me die sooner.

Though one should not be taken in by spurious scientific arguments that running has been proven to prolong life, most of the theories and assumptions that underlie these arguments are reasonable and cogent. Despite the fact that it cannot be proven yet that running helps prevent heart attacks, this does seem to be a reasonable inference from the evidence. One cannot demonstrate scientifically that if a London bus driver started running and lost a few pounds he would live longer, but it would seem to be an intelligent course for him to take. We do know from the evidence that exists from large jogging programs that running would not reduce his life expectancy. We also know that running can play a significant role in rehabilitation of heart patients.

In fact, every runner knows (but cannot prove) that running makes him or her healthier. That this cannot yet be scientifically demonstrated does not invalidate the knowledge. When I was a heavy smoker a number of years ago, I knew that it was an unhealthy habit, though this had not yet been scientifically demonstrated. I could tell by the way my lungs felt when I got up in the morning. Your body will usually let you know what is good for it. It may be wrong on occasion, but unless there is strong evidence to the contrary, the logical course is to believe what it tells you.

The real reason for running, in any event, is that it makes life richer. If it did not it would be a waste of time. There is no question that by keeping active you are more likely to retain the ability to be active as you get older. Nor is there any question in my mind that I would rather be running a marathon like John Kelley as I approach seventy (or fifty or sixty) than spending most of my time sitting around getting stiff. It is the contributions that running can make to your life that are most important, not any delaying effect that it may have on your death. Keep it up!

APPENDIX I

Fasting and Carbohydrate Loading

Two specialized diets are commonly used by serious runners to improve either health or performance. They should probably both be avoided by beginners. Carbohydrate loading unquestionably imposes a good deal of unnecessary stress on the body and is intended by its advocates strictly as a method of improving athletic performance during an important long-distance race. It therefore has no place in the beginner's training. Fasting may be undertaken in preparation for a race too, but its effects and benefits are thought to be more general. It is certainly a less artificial strain. However, I think that it is not advisable to experiment with fasting while you are also trying to accustom your body to the new stress of running. Wait until you have already achieved a good level of fitness before you attempt fasting at the same time. If you want to experiment with a more healthy diet, concentrate on eating more fresh fruits and vegetables or try a vegetarian diet. The following descriptions are intended for runners who are already running many miles each week.

CARBOHYDRATE LOADING

In extended competition one of the limiting factors in performance is the amount of glycogen stored by the muscles that are used in an endurance event; for runners the leg muscles are naturally the ones affected. The distance at which glycogen supplies become depleted depends a lot on the runner's normal training mileage and on many factors that are less well understood. Depletion is only a factor in races of ten miles or more, however, at least among those who train enough to run such races seriously.

Research indicates that if the muscles' glycogen supplies are thoroughly depleted and are then kept low for several days, the muscles will respond by storing a much larger amount of glycogen when supplied with the carbohydrate raw materials. The idea of carbohydrate loading is to time the training during the period preceding an important race and regulate the diet in such a way as to enter the event with the muscles supersaturated with glycogen, thus presumably allowing longer hard racing before entering the glycogen-depletion stage.

A typical schedule for a runner who was carbohydrate loading for a Saturday marathon would be to take a long run the previous Saturday or Sunday at slow or moderate speed. Length would depend on a person's training schedule but would typically be in the twenty-five–thirty-mile range. This run serves to deplete glycogen supplies. The racer would then eat a diet that is very low in carbohydrates for the next three days. For safety this should include sixty grams of carbohydrates a day, but for effectiveness it should not have much more. During this period, training continues at a normal level. The runner will feel very washed out during training because the low-carbohydrate diet does not permit the muscles to replace their depleted glycogen supply. Finally, during the last two or three days before the race, the runner switches to a diet consisting almost entirely of carbohydrates and either stops training or goes to a very low load. A lot of water should be drunk, since the glycogen supercompensation requires it, and several pounds will be gained, due mainly to the extra water bound to the glycogen.

It is worth noting that most of the best marathoners do not go through the full carbohydrate-loading routine, though they may use modified versions. It may be that the diet does not even help those who are putting in enough miles to have extended their collapse points beyond the distance of the race. Note also that regular fasting, loading, or frequent long training runs that deplete glycogen supplies will change the rate at which you go through supercompensation phases so that you may have to cut down the loading period to two days. Bloating, loose bowels, and the loss of the extra pounds you gained while loading are signs that the supercompensation phase has passed.

Carbohydrate loading stresses the body enough so that it should be used only for important races, if at all. On the other hand, until you have experimented with it somewhat, you may not want to risk the full schedule before an important race. The general disruption of routine is more than many racers want to go through before a race. Many racers do follow modifications of the routine, however. One method is to take long, slow runs early in the week while eating fewer carbohydrates than usual to keep the muscles' glycogen supply depleted, finishing with a longish run at midweek. This is followed by a diet emphasizing carbohydrates and a training schedule with reduced mileage. Such a routine will provide a good introduction to loading if you are interested in trying it, before risking the whole regimen preceding a big race.

FASTING

Fasting is used by some racers specifically as a training technique for races in several ways. Regular fasting accustoms the body to glycogen depletion and may train it to use fats more efficiently as fuel. Since little research has been done on the mechanisms involved, explanations are all speculative. We do know that many runners have run well during extended fasts, both during training and races, so it is clear that the body can perform well while fasting, just as it can on a vegetarian diet. Most runners who have tried fasting have felt well and shown no subsequent ill effects. We are talking here generally of fasts lasting from a day to a week or two, though some runners have made longer fasts.

It is clear that nutritionists do not understand how a fasting athlete functions, and many of the accepted strictures are invalid. Runners speculate that maintaining activity during a fast prevents the common effect in starvation diets of losing muscle mass as well as fat. In any case, of the dozens of runners I know who have tried fasting, all of them feel it has made them feel healthier rather than the reverse. Many marathoners regularly fast for twenty-four hours before a long race.

If you decide to try fasting, it is best to make your first few experiments during a period when you are not increasing your training load. Try a one-day fast first, maintaining your normal daily mileage and running as easily and efficiently as you can. Get some experience with shorter fasts before you try a longer one. Some runners fast consuming only water, whereas others prefer to drink fruit juices.

Hunger is not a significant problem while fasting; the common feeling of gnawing in the stomach disappears quickly. True hunger, which is a sensation in the mouth, doesn't begin until you reach the starvation stage, after excess fuel stored in the body has been consumed. Most of us have enough fat stored to last a long time. Mild headaches or lightheadedness lasting a short time are common, but you should feel no other ill effects. Don't try any fasts longer than a week until you have both had a good deal of experience and have researched the subject carefully. The experience of most runners is limited to fasts of a few days.

APPENDIX II

Selected Reading

The main national magazine devoted to running, particularly for people who are out of school, is *Runner's World,* Box 366, Mountain View, California 94040. Membership in the National Jogging Association (NJA) includes a subscription to *The Jogger,* an excellent newsletter. The NJA also carries an excellent stock of running books, many of which are difficult to obtain through normal channels. They will sell to anyone, but they give a 10-percent discount to members. Their address is 1910 K Street, NW 202, Washington, D.C. 20006. The standard periodical for race results and similar reporting is *Track and Field News,* Box 296, Los Altos, California 94022. Another publication emphasizing distance running is *Running Times,* 1816 Lamont Street NW, Washington, D.C. 20010.

Although various pamphlets on individual runners and specialized subjects abound, there are not many general books on running. For beginners interested in the fitness aspects of exercise in general, the old standby is Kenneth Cooper's *Aerobics.* The current version is *The New Aerobics* (New York: Bantam, 1970). Through his administration of programs both for the Air Force and in private life, Cooper has gathered more hard facts on aerobic conditioning than anyone else. His work is the foundation of much of our current knowledge. Another excellent book on fitness in general is *Complete Conditioning,* by David Shepro and Howard Knuttgen (Reading, Mass.: Addison-Wesley, 1975). Their advice is sound and amusing.

Two anthologies on distance running, mainly of articles that appeared originally in *Runner's World,* have been issued by World Publications (which publishes the magazine; same address). They are *The Complete Runner* (1974) and *Guide to Distance Running* (1971). World also publishes some worthwhile reflections on the sport by Joe Henderson, perhaps the best of which is *The Long Run Solution* (1976) and *Dr. Sheehan on Running* (1975), by the always engaging George Sheehan.

The basics of the physiology of running and the training principles derived from it are best summarized in a booklet by David Costill, one of the foremost researchers in the field, *What Research Tells the Coach About Distance Running* (1968); it is put out by the American Alliance for Health, Physical Education, and Recreation, Washington, D.C. 20036. The metabolism of fuels and oxygen is reviewed by E. C. Frederick in the booklet *The Running Body* (New York: World Publications, 1973). The standard text is H. A. De Vries, *Physiology of Exercise for Physical Education and Athletics* (Dubuque, Iowa: Wm. C. Brown Company, 1966).

Those wishing to pursue this subject further might investigate some of the following articles, which should be available at any good library: John A. Faulkner, "New Perspectives in Training for Maximum Performance," *Journal of the American Medical Association,* vol. 205 (1968), pp. 741–46; J. Karlsson, P. O. Åstrand, and B. Ekblom, "Training of the Oxygen Transport System in Man," *Journal of Applied Physiology,* vol. 22 (1967), pp. 1061–65; B. Ekblom et al., "The Effect of Training on Circulatory Response to Exercise," *Journal of Applied Physiology,* vol. 24 (1968), pp. 518–28; Ladislav Novak et al., "Body Composition and Physiologic Function of Athletes," *Journal of the American Medical Association,* vol. 205 (1968), pp. 764–70; Roy Shephard, "The Heart Under the Stress of Olympic Conditions," Ibid., pp. 775–79; Donald Slocum and Stanley James, "Biomechanics of Running," Ibid., pp. 721–28; and E. Buskirk and H. L. Taylor, "Maximal Oxygen Uptake and Its Relation to Body Composition," *Journal of Applied Physiology,* vol. 11 (1957), p. 74.

The best book specifically on running for women is one by Dr. Joan Ullyot, a marathoner who switched to a specialty in exercise physiology after becoming a runner: *Women Running* (New York: World Publications, 1976).

For stretching techniques the two books mentioned in the text are B. K. S. Iyengar, *Light on Yoga* (New York: Schocken, 1966) and Bob Anderson, *Stretching* (P. O. Box 2734, Fullerton, California 92633, 1975). *The Complete Weight Training Book* by Bill Reynolds is published by World. Another good one is John Jesse's *Strength, Power and Muscular Endurance for Runners and Hurdlers* (*Track and Field News*, Box 296, Los Altos, California 94022, 1971).

Running injuries are discussed in a booklet compiled by George Sheehan, *Encyclopedia of Athletic Medicine* (New York: World Publications, 1972). The definitive book on structural problems of the feet and legs as they affect runners is Steven Subotnick's *Podiatric Sports Medicine* (Mount Kisco, New York: Futura, 1975). Subotnick has also written a short book for runners called *The Running Foot Doctor* (New York: World Publications, 1977).

Training is the subject of hundreds of books and pamphlets. The chapters on training in Ron Daws's *The Self-Made Olympian* are outstanding (New York: World Publications, 1977). The most complete book on training is Fred Wilt's *Run Run Run* (*Track and Field News*, 1964). Tom Osler's booklet *The Conditioning of Distance Runners* (*Track and Field News*, 1969) is excellent. An anthology of different racers' comments and training schedules edited by Joe Henderson and entitled *Road Racers and Their Training* was put out by the same publisher in 1970. World Publications has two useful booklets of articles, *Runner's Training Guide* (1973) and *Coaching Distance Runners* (1971).

The original ideas of some of the important coaches and training theorists are published by *Track and Field News* in Percy Cerutty's *Middle Distance Running* (1964) and *Lydiard's Running Training Schedules* (1970). The *Van Aaken Method*, presenting the ideas of the great German doctor, was published by World in 1976. Lydiard's book *Run to the Top* is unfortunately out of print and almost unobtainable.

Besides Daws's book, mentioned above, *Corbitt*, by John Chodes (*Track and Field News*, 1974), the story of one of the great pioneers in American distance running, is well worth reading. Jack Foster's autobiographical booklet *Tale of the Ancient Marathoner* (1974) is delightful.

Index